How MUCH? HOW LITTLE?

How Much Religion May One Have;
How Little May One Have Any At All?

BY

JESSE ARMON BALDWIN

First Fruits Press
Wilmore,
Kentucky c2017

How much? How little? How much religion may one have? How little may one have, to have any at all?
By Jesse Armon Baldwin.

ISBN: 9781621717560 (print), 9781621717577 (digital), 9781621717584 (kindle)

First Fruits Press, © 2017

Digital version at http://place.asburyseminary.edu/firstfruitsheritagematerial/145/

Baldwin, Jesse Armon, 1871-1961.
   How much? How little? How much religion may one have? : how little may one have, to have any at all? / by Jesse Armon Baldwin. – Wilmore, Kentucky: First Fruits Press, ©2017.
      252 pages; cm.
      Reprint. Previously published: Louisville, Ky.: Pentecostal Publishing Company, [192-?].
      ISBN: 9781621717560 (pbk.)
      1. Modernist-fundamentalist controversy. 2. Church history.
      3. Theology, Doctrinal--Popular works. I. Title.
BT82.3.B34 2017   273/.9

Cover design by Jon Ramsay

asburyseminary.edu
800.2ASBURY
204 North Lexington Avenue
Wilmore, Kentucky 40390

First Fruits
THE ACADEMIC OPEN PRESS OF ASBURY SEMINARY

First Fruits Press
The Academic Open Press of Asbury Theological Seminary
204 N. Lexington Ave., Wilmore, KY 40390
859-858-2236
first.fruits@asburyseminary.edu
asbury.to/firstfruits

HOW MUCH? HOW LITTLE?

How Much Religion May One Have;
How Little May One Have to Have Any At All?

BY

JESSE ARMON BALDWIN

LOUISVILLE, KY.
PENTECOSTAL PUBLISHING COMPANY

To the Faculty and Students of the Southern Industrial Institute, Charlotte, North Carolina, 1901-1926, and to all others who had a part in that beautiful work for and with young people, this book is affectionately dedicated.

TABLE OF CONTENTS

Africaner.

Foreword

Some years ago I had some business with a banker friend in an important city in another state. The business finished, he turned to me and said, "If you had to teach a Sunday school class of eighty-five men next Sunday what would you say?" I happened to be familiar with the lesson and proceeded to a discussion of it. In a little while he stopped me until he could get a pad and pencil. He expressed himself as being pleased and insisted that I write it out and publish it in a book. He explained that what he liked about it especially was that it threw light on a situation that had worried him. He said he had on his Board of Directors a man who was just one of the finest men he ever saw. He felt that if in the next world anyone should be worthy to take a joyful place with the redeemed this man would. But he professed a creed quite different from his own, therefore did not possess the kind of faith in Jesus as Saviour that some passages in the Bible seemed to require. As an Elder in the Presbyterian Church, and as a teacher in the Sunday school, he had not been able to find a solution to his problem.

I have come in touch with many others who for various reasons were disturbed about questions of a more or less similar nature. So, now after some years of consideration, I am endeavoring to write out some thoughts that may enable others to secure a more satisfying faith both as to their own spiritual condition, and that of their loved ones as well.

In the treatment of this subject it has been necessary to give a brief review of the history of the Christian Church. It has been seen that individuals and the Church as a whole have sometimes seemed almost to lose entirely the divine touch. At other times, spiritual heights have been reached for which no earthly explanation could be given.

It has been very apparent that spiritual power in the Church has been opposed by materialism in all ages, but that it reached its most malignant aspects just before the Reformation. It has not been so apparent, but it seems clear enough when stated, that together with the material, and in large measure because of it, there has been a determined fight against the supernatural. This, for the most part, has taken three forms:

1. A denial of the inspiration of the Bible.
2. A denial of the deity of Christ.
3. Not so much a verbal denial of, but an almost total neglect to recognize the deity of the Holy Spirit, and a failure to seek and receive His help.

There have been three periods during which this has been peculiarly distressing and hurtful: Arianism in the fourth century; deism in the eighteenth century; and modernism in the twentieth century. In each of the periods the spiritual tone and condition of the world became very low, but the world emerged from the first two. We are in the third, modernism, today. In order to get out, three things are necessary: we must work and fight and pray. Our task lies before us, is even at our door.

Underlying all discussion and thinking on these subjects, we must not forget the fact that becomes clearly evident to one who reads the Bible; that the Bible is

a supernatural book, and that Christianity is a supernatural religion.

I have carefully refrained from the use of theological terms and any expressions that would be unfamiliar
to any intelligent reader.

Charlotte 7, N. C.   J. A. BALDWIN.

Introduction

Religion includes the relationship of man to God, and of man to each other. It is, therefore, a very comprehensive word, because it includes or contacts every relationship of life. This is true whether we welcome the fact, or resent its intrusion into our thinking, and have a feeling of indignation that it persists in demanding a large place in our most secret thoughts. In this volume, as in common usage, "religion" is used in the restricted sense of *right* relationship to God and man.

The special reason that it demands and has such a large place in our thinking is because of the insistent belief that these relationships will not cease with this life, but will continue throughout eternity. Nor is it about ourselves alone that we are concerned, but about our loved ones as well. Indeed most people who can be considered pious are more concerned about their loved ones than about themselves. Then too, in the case of all good people there is no little concern about the spiritual condition of the masses of the people of the earth.

Will most of these people in some way find an entrance into the better world, or will the vast multitudes of earth be eternally separated from God? Whether from genuine interest or idle speculation such questions must come to every thoughtful mind.

A layman said he had had three ministers. The first thought most of the people would finally be lost and he was greatly troubled about it. The second thought nearly everybody would go to hell, and he seemed to be glad of it. They were a tough, ornery lot who would not listen to the preacher, and would not try to live right, and they would simply get what they deserved. The third was uneasy about all of us, but simply hoped for the best.

There are groups throughout the world, some small, others very large, who think they have a monopoly of the favor of God, that their group alone will enjoy the delights of the heavenly world, and that all the others will be cast into the outer darkness. The most pronounced case of that sort I ever came into personal contact with was a Negro preacher to whom I gave a ride near my native heath. He belonged to that small group who take the words of Jesus literally as to the washing of feet. I soon found that he thought that anybody would have little chance of entering the pearly gates who did not literally wash the feet of others in church. It may be said that such narrowness is not confined to the poor and ignorant. It would be ludicrous in many cases if it were not so serious. On the other hand, there are those who believe that God is too good and merciful to permit any of His creatures to suffer forever.

These are great and vital questions. They are entirely too important to be settled by a few isolated proof texts—passages that may not bear on this particular point at all. But in order to get a satisfactory conception of the subject the Bible as a whole must be permitted to tell its own story.

HOW GOD HAS REVEALED HIMSELF TO MAN

How God Has Revealed Himself to Man

The principal means by which God has revealed Himself to man have been:

1. By direct speech.
2. Through dreams and visions.
3. By the ministry of angels.
4. Through His recorded messages in the Bible.
5. By the forces of nature.
6. By His special providences.
7. By the life and ministry of Jesus.
8. By the Holy Spirit, using the above named agencies, and also acting directly and personally.

Treating these more fully:

1. *God Speaks Directly To Man.*

In the early period of the human race it was important for God to speak directly to the individuals. He used the form of expression that best met the need. Therefore, He spoke to Adam and Eve; to Enoch and Noah; later to Abraham because he would listen to the voice of God, and hearing, obey. He probably talked directly more to Moses than to anyone else, for the double reason that he had such an enormous task in leading the children of Israel to the Promised Land, and because the time had come for God's will and purpose to be recorded. To many others He spoke directly, especially the prophets. In recent ages there being so many other agencies for conveying His messages there are few records of direct speech. But if there is real need He speaks still in a voice that can be heard with natural hearing.

It was my privilege years ago to see and hear that great missionary to India, Rev. Jacob Chamberlain. He told the story of a most remarkable experience he had in India. He and his party, including guides, were traveling through a flooded section of India during the rainy season. With deep waters on almost every side they became lost. They were greatly perplexed as to what course to pursue. A mistaken route would prove serious, if not fatal. Just then he heard a voice as though coming out of the sky, "Turn to the left at the Godavery (River)." That was not at all in accordance with the views and advice of the guides. He heeded the Voice and not the guides, and later information showed that that had been the only possible salvation for them.

Another case was that of Rev. James L. Kennedy, another notable missionary, who gave sixty years of consecrated service to Brazil. In 1909 he came near drowning in the Atlantic. Of this event he says that as he struggled against the might of the waves trying to reach the shore, the word of the Lord came to him as plainly as the words of a fellowman, "Young man, you have not yet finished your work." Believing it certainly the word of God, he relaxed and soon the waves rolled him to the shore.

Again, a good woman in this country was left a widow with a half a dozen little children on a small farm. One morning after she had gotten the children off to school, the agony of the struggle pressed down upon her, and she sobbed out the words, "No one cares for me." Immediately from behind her came the words spoken plainly, "He careth for thee." She looked around to see who spoke, but there was no one in or about the house. Her load fell off and she went about her duties with a light heart. So sacred was the occasion that excepting one time she never told it till in her eighty-fifth year on a dying bed. But she said that there was perhaps never a day that she had not thought of it, and because of it felt a constantly renewed strength for her difficult duties.

ANGELIC MESSENGERS

To deliver messages and render other service God has made very frequent use of angels. The instances of this service are exceedingly numerous. I will mention two well known cases. Peter was in prison, and plans had been made for his death on the morrow. "But prayer was made without ceasing of the Church unto God for him. And, behold, the angel of the Lord came upon him, and a light shined in the prison; and he smote Peter on the side and raised him up, saying, arise up quickly. And his chains fell off his hands. And the angel said unto him, Gird thyself, and bind on thy sandals. And so he did, and He saith unto him, Cast thy garment about thee, and follow me. And he went out and followed Him; and wist not that it was true which was done by the angel; but thought he saw a vision. When they were past the first and second ward, they came to the iron gate which opened to them of his own accord; and they went out, and passed on through one street, and forthwith the angel departed from him."

Then there was that dramatic scene in the life of St. Paul, who with other prisoners was being carried across the Mediterranean Sea to Rome. They had left a port against the advice of Paul. Soon after a terrific storm arose and continued many days. They were exceedingly tossed with the tempest, and all hope of being saved was taken away. But after long abstinence Paul stood forth in the midst of them (276 in all) and said, "Sirs, ye should have harkened unto me, and not have loosed from Crete, and to have gained this harm and loss. And now I exhort you to be of good cheer, for there shall be no loss of any man's life among you, but of the ship. For there stood by me this night the angel of God, whose I am, and whom I serve, saying, 'Fear not, Paul; thou must be brought to Cæsar; and lo, God hath given thee all them that sail with thee.' Wherefore, Sirs, be of good cheer, for I believe God, that it shall be even as it was told me." And so it was.

In modern times God uses other means of communication more than through angels, at least in visible form. Here, however, it was my privilege in my early ministry to know of one very clear case. It occurred in the family of a man who later became one of my most intimate friends. A daughter of this friend was very sick. Her husband, named Henry, had died two years previously. They were both very consecrated Christians. Now it was nearing her time to pass over and join him on the other side. Just before the last, her eyes brightened and with joy she reached out her hands and said, "Henry!" Then she talked on and said, "There

are the angels, don't you see them?" And pointed out
in front. There was not a particle of doubt in the
minds of those who saw and heard her that day but
that she saw her husband and a group of angels. I was
not present at that time, but just before and shortly
thereafter, and there has never been any doubt in my
mind but that God had done His faithful servant the
signal honor of sending her husband and a band of
angels to convoy her to her eternal home.

VISIONS AND DREAMS

Visions and dreams are indicative of the activity of
the subconscious mind. Most dreams do not have any
special significance. But throughout the ages men and
women have here and there had dreams that they were
satisfied had a meaning for them. Dreams have generally been short and definite, while visions have been
longer and generally with some directions for future
activity. A good many prophetic messages were received in visions. When sent of God they were for a
definite purpose. Joseph's dream no doubt brought
him comfort in many a dark hour. The visions of
Peter and Cornelius were longer and more specific, and
were needed particularly at that time when the Jews
needed to change their attitude towards others.

GOD'S PROVIDENCES

David learned during a year of troubled days and
sleepless nights, and years of other evil effects in home
and kingdom that the way of the transgressor is hard.
Paul through a thorn in the flesh learned that even
with the deepest spiritual experiences there may be a
place for suffering in life's development. No one can
ever know in how many ways and in what ways God is

speaking from sick beds, from thwarted ambitions, from disappointed hopes, from blasted aspirations. But His children have found by experience that these help to make us conscious of God, and render us readier to listen to His voice.

NATURE

"The heavens declare the glory of God, and the earth showeth His handiwork." It has often been noted that astronomers are usually devout men. The stars in their courses not only fight for the righteous, but they convey to their earthly searchers something of the greatness and majesty of God. Sidney Lanier learned the same lesson from the marsh hen in the marshes of Glynn as she built her nest on the watery sod, and this inspired him to have for the foundation of his life the greatness of God. So it is that from the starry heavens to the mire of earth God speaks to us. This message is ever present with us by day and by night. Roaring waterfalls, raging rivers, turbulent seas, destructive storms and terrific thunders may indicate something of the severity of God's wrath; the beautiful green and variegated panorama of earth's changing seasons and the inexpressible grandeur of the starry heavens reveal something of the gentleness of His mercy.

In addition to these general influences the direct and specific influences are numerous. The best known, perhaps, is the effect produced on Luther by a storm. A young law student with brilliant prospects, he was passing through a forest when a very severe electrical storm came up. Balls of lightning rolled in front of him, and the crash of the storm was on every side. In prostration before God he promised Him if He would spare him he would devote himself to His service. Peace and quiet reigned again, but Luther remained true to his promise. He gave up the brilliant prospects in law, and the hope that his father had for him of a marriage of wealth, and took the vows of a mendicant monk. God needed Luther for a great work, and Luther needed special training for that work. The storm played a most important part in it all.

THE BIBLE

"Thy word is a lamp unto my feet and a light unto my path." As a guide-post at every cross-roads the Bible has played a mighty part in the journey heavenward of most good people. Nature started Luther aright, but it was God's word that was the determining factor in making him the great religious leader that he came to be. Groping pitifully in the fogs of uncertainty a passage from the Bible brought joy to his troubled heart. "The just shall live by faith." Not, then, by saying prayers, not by starving himself sick, not by humiliating beggary, not by great gifts or pilgrimages, not by the aid of the accumulated merit produced by the prayers of saints—no, by none of these, but by simple faith in God—something that is possible for the lowest, something that is always available for the highest. This was the immediate inauguration of Luther into his heroic struggles and glorious victories for a purer, better world.

JESUS

Jesus was a messenger of God, but much more, He was the Message. He was pre-eminently God's Word or Message to man. Satan convinced Adam that God

did not love him, that in fact He was withholding something from man that he was entitled to have, and having, he would be wiser and happier. Adam believed
Satan and was thus deceived. God sent messengers to
men, as He could secure messengers and hearers, to
correct that lie. The result was but a very partial success. Finally He sent His Son. That would be a Message they could not fail to hear. He revealed all necessary truth in His teachings, emphasized by His deeds.
But above all, He showed the world how God could and
did live. That example as well as His words, work and
sacrificial death, is a precious heritage to us who would
follow in His steps. It is of interest to note that during
His public ministry there is no record of any other
revelation of God to men except that connected with
Him. None other was needed, but they were frequent
both before and after.

THE HOLY SPIRIT

The Holy Spirit cooperates with and directs or em-
phasizes all the above named forces, and perhaps others that we know not of. But in addition He acts directly on the human mind and heart. He said to the
saints of Antioch, "Separate me Barnabas and Saul for
the work whereunto I have called them." Later, as
Paul was going through Asia Minor, and came near to
the Province of Asia of which Ephesus was the Capital,
he planned to go there. But he was forbidden of the
Holy Ghost to do so at that time. Going forward a
little he decided to go through Bithynia, but the Spirit
suffered him not. Being thus forbidden to go to the left
or to the right there was nothing to do but go forward.

So he came to the town of Troas on the sea. He was evidently greatly perplexed as to the next step and was earnestly praying over the matter. Then there came the vision in which there appeared a man of Macedonia saying, "Come over into Macedonia and help us." Paul did not know it but there lay before him a vast field of service. He took ship and departed for Macedonia, and there laid the foundations for the Christian Church in Europe, and from there it came much later to America. Most of us have but slight appreciation of the fact that "The spirit maketh intercession for us with groanings that cannot be uttered," and whenever we will let Him, He will guide our footsteps as He did those of St. Paul.

THREE DISPENSATIONS OF GRACE

Three Dispensations of Grace

While God has revealed Himself as just indicated it becomes clear with a careful consideration that God's revelations to man did not come all at once, but at different times through a long period; that there were three distinct stages or levels of revelation. These may be called dispensations of grace as follows:

1. The dispensation of the Father.
2. The dispensation of the Son.
3. The dispensation of the Holy Spirit.

The dispensation of the Father extends from the beginning to the baptism of Jesus.

The dispensation of the Son from the baptism of Jesus to pentecost.

The dispensation of the Holy Spirit from pentecost to the second coming of the Lord.

The dispensation of the Father was characterized by fear, as of a good but stern father. "Fear God and keep His commandments," is the Biblical representation of this period.

The dispensation of the Son was characterized by peace. Jesus said to His followers during His active ministry, "My peace I give unto you."

The dispensation of the Holy Spirit was characterized by joy. "Rejoice evermore" represents the high water mark of spiritual experience.

The Bible gives us a very varied account of each of these dispensations.

THE DISPENSATION OF THE FATHER

The dispensation of the Father has a very extensive representation of religious experience, especially because the Old Testament in its entirety is taken up with it. The biographical element in it is very full and instructive. Unlike most biographies the bad as well as the good is plainly given. As a mental and spiritual laboratory it is emphatically in a class by itself. We are taken behind the scenes, not as a special favor, but as though it is the perfectly natural thing to do. The stories are so simply and at the same time superbly told that it scarcely occurs to the reader to marvel at the spiritual revelations.

During all the earlier part of the period covered by the dispensation of the Father the people had no Bible. Jesus and the Holy Spirit were existent, of course, but had not come in their official capacity. The people were not yet ready for the ministry that they would come to give. The people as a whole had but slight knowledge of God compared with what may be known now. But it is very important for us to know that though Jesus had not come to the earth in the flesh, and though He had not yet died for a lost world, nevertheless it was through the shedding of His blood that we are saved now not only but by the same sacrifice all those in the earlier period had the same privilege. That is the meaning of blood sacrifices. That is the explanation of Leviticus. *The voluntary sacrifice of Jesus was accepted before the deed in order that all men during all time might find in Him salvation even as we who have come later.* The test of faith that was given in the earlier period was the offering of animal sacrifices.

However, every individual or generation or race had the benefit of His death even though they did not know about and could not exercise this test of their faith. It is apparent that during this period the knowledge of God was very limited. Were the great masses of the people in rebellion against God, or were they in the dispensation of the Father? This is a matter of general interest so far as the people of that time is concerned, but a matter of vital importance to people today in heathen lands, and in our own land to those who for any reason have but a slight or perturbed knowledge of God. Let us look somewhat into the inward lives of some of the people of that dispensation.

Noah was the best man of his time, "a just man and perfect in his generation, and Noah walked with God." But after the flood he drank too much wine and was drunken. Abraham was one of the greatest men our earth has produced, a man whom God could trust. But on two or three occasions his conduct would not be considered worthy of a devout Christian of our time. Then there was Judah, who was head of the tribe that became the greatest and most influential of the twelve tribes. His conduct in sexual matters was such that it would bring a religious leader of our time into disgrace. Even Moses killed a man, and it was a homicide that could scarcely be justified by Christian standards.

The story told in the 19th chapter of Judges indicates a widespread degradation almost beyond belief. If the Bible were not inspired it would scarcely have told that gruesome story. They would have found some other reason for the small numbers of the tribe of Benjamin, or at least would have glossed over that painful and pathetic story.

But there is another story of the same period told us in the Book of Ruth, one of the most beautiful stories in all literature. The simple account gives us an insight into the homelife of Canaan and Moab. It unfolds the beautiful life of two noble women, mother-in-law and daughter-in-law. It reveals a kindly community life where the stranger within the gates receives a gracious welcome; it portrays a relationship between employer and employee seldom seen even in our day; it closes with a pretty romance in which a true man and a lovely young woman are married, and become the ancestors of a distinguished line whose labors and influence have throughout the ages since enriched the world. May we not express the hope that this story rather than the other is more representative of the entire people? May that not mean that the number in the dispensation of the Father was much larger than that of those in rebellion against God?

In that early period while many of the peoples had drifted so far away from God that they ceased to hold in memory and in reverence the need for blood sacrifices, they never got away from some realization of a higher power, and of their obligation to worship Him. Having lost the revelation handed down through the generations as to the knowledge of the character of God, they let their imagination run riot in forming unworthy images and representations of Him. So idolatry became common. But in their most imperfect way they did pay reverence to a power greater than themselves.

The descendants of Israel were more faithful to Jehovah than any other nation of the world, and yet these as a whole represented a low standard. Idolatry permitted a hurtful gratification of appetites and passions, and Jehovah did not. There was no difference between the nations in this respect except in degree. In every nation there were those who were measurably faithful to the best and highest that they knew. But the proportion was larger in Israel than in the other nations. Indeed in most nations the knowledge of one true God, pure and holy, seemed almost to have faded away. But in Israel that knowledge was kept alive by prophets and others. So this people remained the center of pure worship throughout the generations.

We know more of the conflict of the forces of good and evil in Israel than in the other nations. But we know much of the other nations through references in the Bible, classical and other literature, archæology, artifacts, and traditions. These sources reveal much that is corrupt, and also not a little that is true and beautiful. Especially do the sacred books of the Hindus and Persians indicate that there has been a serious degeneration since those books were written, as there had been at that time a degeneration from an earlier period.

It has generally been assumed that wars have been prevalent almost from the beginning. Very able prehistorians now tell us that it is not true. For a long period there was no war. When war did come it greatly checked the development of the peoples of the world. Then, too, slavery was for the most part in the early period the result of war. The conquered people were made slaves, and the slaves were often more intelligent than the masters.

There have been in all ages and among all peoples certain recognized standards of right and wrong. Truthfulness, dependability, and reliability have been

recognized as important. Kindliness has always been a
key to every kind of heart. Everywhere there have
been sexual standards though these have varied greatly at different times and among different peoples.

Where was the dividing line between those for
God and those against Him? Were they only to enter
into the presence of God and enjoy His companionship
forever who verbally professed to know Him and be
His followers? I cannot think so. Of course, at this
period Jesus had not come to earth in the flesh and they
could not speak in His name. Only a small number
understood the significance of bloody sacrifices in an-
ticipation of Him who should die for the sins of the
world.

We know that their knowledge of God was very limited. We can know but little of their consecration and
faith. A verbal test would mean little. The determining test would be *attitude*—their attitude to God,
or we might say, their attitude towards the highest and
best that they knew. If obedience and reverence represented their attitude they would be in the dispensation of the Father. But if their attitude was one of rebellion they then could have no place in the company
of those who love and trust Him.

As a young minister I talked frequently with an
old gentleman who had been an able and successful
lawyer and a distinguished judge with an enviable
record for fairness and justice. Though a member of
the church and of excellent habits he did not have a
consciousness of the forgiveness of his sins, and he was
seriously troubled about it. At a political convention
a friend in an adjoining room in a hotel heard him

through a thin partition praying pathetically: "Lord, be merciful to me a sinner." He sought help from any individual or book that gave promise of relief. But so far as I know he went into unconsciousness and death without an assurance of pardon.

He was evidently not in the dispensation of the Son. Was he in the dispensation of the Father? Jesus described God to us so anyone can understand Him. He simply used the word, "Father." Can we think of a wise and good father seeing at his door the outstretched hand and hearing the pleading voice for mercy of a son, however wayward he may have been, and turn from him in anger, or kick him out without pity? So I think we may say on the authority of Jesus the same for our heavenly Father.

Is a disposition to sin inherited? Instead of attempting to treat this in terms of theology, may we not secure a more satisfactory understanding of the matter by an examination of the divinely inspired human laboratory, the Bible? Sin encourages us to go in the line of least resistance; God, often, if not always, demands that we go the more difficult way. It would, doubtless, have been much easier for Abraham to stay in the city of Ur than to go out into a new land, not knowing whither he went. Jacob tried the easy way of getting what things he wanted—the way of trickery and deceit; but it was harmful to him and displeasing to God. Joseph had one of the severest of tests. Though a slave, he was in charge of a fine home, the mistress of which used all her seductive powers upon him for evil. But he chose the hard way—the way of purity and resistance, even though he was put in jail because of it. Moses had for his own practically everything the world had to offer—power, wealth, social prestige—but he

determined upon the hard way, and went out into the
wilderness and became a common laborer. But we do
not have to go back to ancient times for illustrations.
They are all about us today. In order not to drift with
the current into disaster the people that we come into
contact with daily have to struggle constantly against
the current if they would live noble lives. They must
often refuse to be dominated by pride, lust, avarice or
hate. In every life there are decisions that have to be
made, and there is an urge, whether yielded to or not,
to go in the line of least resistance and for the bad. It
can scarcely be denied that the taint of sin is there, but
it is comforting to know that no one is condemned except for sins knowingly and willingly committed. So
we may say that the taint of sin has been in every life
and therefore inherited. If that is so, and if to serve
God necessitates traveling the hard way, why should
anyone willingly undertake to travel that road at all?
Why should anyone willingly enter into the dispensation of the Father and especially into the higher dispensations? There are three reasons: First, each of us
has a conscience that continually prompts us to go the
right way, though it may be a way of difficulty, and
disturbs us when we would go the way of evil, though
that seems easy and delightful. Second, when sufficient maturity has come to us we can look about us and
see the beneficent results of right doing on the one
hand and the distressing results of evil doing on the
other. Third, there is a firm conviction that God stands
by and helps those who disdain the easy way, and
steadfastly turn their faces toward Him, and that this,
though intangible and invisible, is the most effective

help in all the universe. We may definitely say that all the power of the Godhead is available for him who is traveling the road of righteousness. This power is so readily available and is so effective in transforming the lives of men that it is possible through it for men to reach such spiritual heights that they may become but little lower than God.

THE DISPENSATION OF THE SON

Why, it may be asked, did Jesus delay so long His coming? It was because the world was not yet ready for Him. But now when the strong Roman Government made possible reasonable safety for her citizens, and frequent intercourse among the nations; when the land of Canaan, long an isolated spot, had become the center of the nations; when the beautiful Greek language had made communication possible among the cultured of all nations; when the philosophies of the world had failed to satisfy, and it had become certain that man by searching could not find God; when the masses of the people were oppressed with a never-ceasing heartache, then it was, in the fullness of time, that God sent forth His Son. Larger privileges were just about to be granted to the human race. Jesus, the Son of God, came as a little human baby. He grew up, and at thirty years of age entered upon His public ministry. He went to be baptized of John, immediately after which the Spirit of God descended like a dove and lighted upon Him, and a voice from Heaven said, "This is my beloved Son in whom I am well pleased." Thus Jesus inaugurated a new religious epoch, the dispensation of the Son. It was all very quiet. There was no flare of trumpets. It was not a mass movement. Individuals singly or in small groups gathered about Him and heard Him talk. The first conversation mentioned is of peculiar interest. Soon after His baptism John the Baptist stood and two of His disciples; looking upon Jesus as He walked, he saith, "Behold the Lamb of God," and the two disciples heard him speak, and followed Jesus. One of the two was Andrew, the other almost certainly John. They went with Jesus to where He was stopping and spent the day with Him. What a day it must have been! How we would have loved to listen in! We do not know what was said, but we do know the effect. These two men were convinced that Jesus was the One for whom they had been looking. Each went out and brought his brother to Jesus, and so the process has gone on through the ages. They received from Jesus a peace of heart, a calmness of spirit, an exaltation of feeling, a certainty of religious experience they had never known before. And they were glad to tell others about it.

It seems more than probable that all these men had been in the dispensation of the Father. The mother of John and James was a sister of Mary, the mother of Jesus. We would not naturally expect them to have hearts of rebellion against God. It seems certain that Nathaniel was a good man, for Jesus Himself said of him, "An Israelite indeed in whom is no guile." So, with many, if not all of His earliest disciples, it was not a case of getting right with God for the first time, but rather of getting on a higher landing place of the stairway that leads to God. If we get this fact clearly in mind it will help us to understand other important questions that may arise. But it is not likely that everyone who came to Jesus came first into the dispensation of the Father. Instead it seems quite certain that some who had never yielded their lives to God at all were so charmed by His words and His personality, and so desirous of having what His followers seemed to have, that they went to Him at once from a condition of rebellion against God to a complete acceptance of Jesus, of simple faith in Him.

The means of entering into this new dispensation was faith—"He that believeth in me." In later years Paul proclaimed, "Believe in the Lord Jesus Christ and thou shalt be saved." It was a most wonderful experience of the increasing numbers who came to Jesus, and yielded their lives to Him. But He made it perfectly clear that to follow Him was no simple, easy matter. "Believing in Jesus" were not magical words, as so many people have since seemed to think. The real meaning is that we believe in His way of life, that we think as He does, that we are willing, if need be, to give up wealth, (or forego the possibility of it) and friends, and loved ones in order to live the Jesus way. The rich young ruler came to Jesus. He wanted what Jesus had to give. His attitude towards Jesus was reverent. He would have been glad to use those words that sound so beautiful, "I believe." But Jesus would not permit him to have a misconception about so important a point. If he would look out upon a world of sin and suffering as Jesus did he could not continue to live the self-indulgent life he was living. He would have to get out and share his wealth, and share his learning, and share his pleasing personality. That was a price he was not willing to pay, and he went away sorrowful. And we do not even know his name. Some years later another rich young ruler was struggling with the same problems. It came to the point with him whether Jesus was really the Son of God. When it came to that Jesus opened the windows of heaven to satisfy the yearning, questioning heart. And the name Paul has been a household word in Christendom for nearly two thousand years. How Jesus did yearn that everybody in the world would believe on Him, that they would look on others as He did—with compassion, that they would be willing to pour out their lives for others as He was doing; and then that they might in turn receive in their hearts the peace that passeth all understanding. Hear His pleading voice: "Come unto me, all ye that labor and are heavy laden, and I will give you rest. Take my yoke upon you, and learn of me; for I am meek and lowly of heart, and ye shall find rest unto your souls. For my yoke is easy and my burden is light."

The distinction between the dispensation of the Father and that of the Son was brought out especially in one who was very close to our Lord, his kinsman in the flesh and His forerunner, John the Baptist. That was a wonderful tribute Jesus paid him: "Among them that are born of woman there hath not arisen a greater than John the Baptist." Heroic Elijah was not greater, nor the thoughtful Jeremiah, nor even the seraphic Isaiah. But Jesus goes on to say, "Notwithstanding he that is least in the Kingdom of God (or the Kingdom of heaven) is greater than he." Now what could Jesus have meant there except that the least in the dispensation of the Son (as herein explained) was greater than the highest in the dispensation of the Father? Not as the world would count greatness, but of a wider spiritual horizon, of deeper spiritual experience, of fuller understanding of divine things. One would naturally ask if at the baptism of Jesus, John did not come into the dispensation of the Son. What he saw and heard there no doubt brought him awe and amazement. But not yet, it seems, did there come that peace which passeth all understanding. Later, in the dark dungeons of Machærus, his soul was troubled and he sent some of his disciples to Jesus to ask him if He was indeed the One for whom they had been looking. There are few occasions in the life of Jesus, if any, when he showed greater tenderness. He told the messengers to stand by Him, and as they stood a procession of blind, crippled, diseased in mind and body passed by, and at His word health and strength came again. We may be sure that while He was interested in every afflicted, broken body that received His healing touch, He was even more interested in that heroic prophet down in the dungean of Machærus. Each person changed from the helplessness and hopelessness of disease to the vigor and buoyancy of health was a part of the message that the messengers carried back to John. At last He turned to the messengers and said: "Go tell John what you have seen and heard;" then, reminiscent of Isaiah He added, "And tell him the poor have the gospel preached to them." It was enough. Faith in Jesus drove the black demons of despair from John's heart, as he passed, I think, beyond any doubt from the dispensation of the Father into the dispensation of the Son. The headman's axe now had no terror for him, and a short time later when it fell we may be well assured that for him there was light.

What marvelous days those were for the little band that did believe in Him as they walked with Him through the hills and vales of Judea and Galilee! "Never man spake like this man." In a disturbed world it was always calm at His side.

Then there came a time when Jesus tried to tell them that He would soon leave them. But they could not believe it. They did not see how they could get on without Him. If some of us who have come to know Jesus as our best friend were to come face to face with the fact or fear that we might lose Him how our hearts would be filled with sorrow, as their's were!

But now Jesus made the most astounding statement that they had ever heard fall from His lips: "It is expedient for you that I go away." Jesus not merely told the truth, He was the Truth. But how could this be true? That little group came to have a personal knowledge of the truth of this statement, as have untold thousands of others throughout the ages. But that knowledge came later, and now sorrow filled their hearts. Sorrowful days, terrible days followed! He died and was buried. But He broke the bonds of the tomb, and came out conqueror of death, and the grave. But even this, though the mightiest of all miracles, was not what Jesus was speaking of. Jesus said the Holy Spirit would come, and told them to remain in Jerusalem and not to undertake to carry out His instructions until He did come.

THE DISPENSATION OF THE HOLY SPIRIT

Fifty days after the resurrection and ten days after the final ascension of Jesus, and after about 120 men and women had been praying together for ten days, a most remarkable thing occurred. "Suddenly there came a sound from heaven as of a rushing, mighty wind, and it filled all the house where they were sitting and there appeared unto them cloven tongues like as of fire, and it sat upon each of them. And they were all filled with the Holy Ghost." This experience brought to them a joy that they had never in their most vivid imagination thought possible; it gave them a courage that was not merely for a short period but proved to be abiding through days and months and years of pain, struggle, and difficulty.

It equipped them in a marvelous way for their work. Their immediate task, opportunity, and privilege was to tell of this glorious experience to the multitudes in Jerusalem, assembled from different countries and speaking many different languages. Immediately they were given the power to tell the story to each man of the many nationalities then present in Jerusalem in his own language, so he might get at first hand the blessed story of that day. Thus another religious epoch was inaugurated.

Jesus had voluntarily placed upon Himself some of the limitations of humanity. But now He sends the Holy Spirit upon whom there were no such limitations. This dispensation is characterized especially by an experience of inward joy, and manifestation of outward courage. The freshness of the first morning was not gone before a remarkable exhibition of courage was manifested before the vast multitude. Peter, but lately so cowardly that he trembled before a servant girl, now speaks out to the leading citizens of Jerusalem, and speaking of Jesus said, "Ye have taken and by wicked hands have crucified and slain my Lord." There have been multiplied instances of such courage from that notable hour throughout the ages to this day.

A little later Paul and Silas gave an inspiring example of inward joy in spite of pain and unjust treatment. A girl possessed with a spirit of divination brought her masters much gain. Paul cast out the evil spirit, and thus incurred the hostility of her masters. These succeeded in having Paul and Silas beaten with many stripes, and cast into prison. This was as little conducive to joy as one could very well imagine. And yet in the inner prison, with their feet fast in the stocks, and no doubt the blood flowing from the wounds made by the lash and drying on their back, at midnight Paul and Silas prayed and sang praises to God. No wonder God ordered an earthquake to shake loose their bonds, open the doors of the prison, and set His faithful servants free!

These two illustrations are very marked but not isolated cases. Multitudes throughout the ages with a like courage have shown a skeptical world that they hold not their lives dear unto themselves. Their Lord who will not let Himself be indebted to His children even for a cup of cold water given to one of the least of earth's children in His name has graciously poured into their hearts a joy and gladness not of this world.

In the days immediately after Pentecost there were those who had received this wonderful blessing of the baptism of the Holy Spirit, and were therefore in the new and higher dispensation, that of the Holy Spirit. That number, however, was at first small. There was a

larger number who had come to know Jesus and to believe in Him. Through faith in Him there had come to
them a sweet peace. That number, though larger than
those who had received the baptism of the Holy Spirit,
was also small. The great mass of the peoples of the
world was in neither of these two groups. Now we
ask: Was every man, woman, and child who did not belong to one of these two groups a sinner, separated from
God, and in rebellion against Him? Nay, nay, we cannot think so. Before Jesus came they had a place of
hope. Yea, some of them enjoyed many spiritual privileges. The fact that now larger opportunities were
theirs for the asking (if they knew how and where
and whom to ask) did not deprive them of the opportunities they already had. As the years went by more
people received the baptism of the Holy Ghost, but so
far as we can tell the number has never been large.
The number who believed in Christ as Saviour and
Lord was much larger, but compared with the number
who did not profess such faith was not at all large.

A very large part of the earth's population throughout the ages have belonged to groups different from
the two groups just considered. Are all of these outside
the pale of safety? Is there no spiritual hope for them?
No salvation for them now, or ever? According to
some they cannot be saved, because they have not complied with the conditions of salvation. Jesus said,
(John 3:18) "He that believeth on Him is not condemned but he that believeth not is condemned already, because he hath not believed in the name of the
only begotten Son of God." Believing in Jesus, then,
is the test of discipleship. But what does it mean to be-

lieve in Him? Are these magic words; and if we say
them over and over have we complied with the conditions of salvation? If it were that simple people could
sail over to the eternal shore on gliders. It is not that
simple. Believing in Jesus means looking on life as
Jesus does; having a feeling of compassion for others as
He has; loving righteousness as He does; hating false-
hood, and injustice, and cruelty as He does. But if we
do not so look on life; if we do not have the attitude towards others that is requisite for salvation, what provision is there for securing such attitude? That is the
heart of the world's greatest problem. All other problems beside it are insignficant. The answer is that Jesus secured that for us by the voluntary sacrifice of
Himself. That fact is so generally recognized by Christians that there is no need for argument. But there are
two collateral questions the answers to which are not
so clearly recognized:

First: How was anyone saved at all before Christ
made His sacrifice? HOW WERE ADAM AND ABRA-
HAM AND ISAIAH AND OTHERS SAVED? WE
ANSWER THAT THOUGH THEY DID NOT UNDER-
STAND IT CLEARLY, THOUGH INDEED THEY DID
NOT KNOW ABOUT IT AT ALL; NEVERTHELESS
IT WAS ALREADY ACCOMPLISHED IN THEIR BE-
HALF IN THE HEART OF GOD. THAT WAS GOD'S
PLAN AND THEIR SALVATION DEPENDED UPON
THEIR WILLING ACCEPTANCE OF THAT PLAN.

Second: The next question is one about which
there had not been a generally accepted answer. What
provision, if any, is there for the multitudes since
Christ, for the multitudes today, who do not know Jesus

and have never taken the pledge of allegiance to Him? The answer to this question will evolve from our further study.

Each of these dispensations includes a wide range of experience because of the differences in knowledge, consecration and faith. This in addition to the great differences of the three dispensations themselves. Just here let us emphasize one fact generally overlooked *All three dispensations may and often do exist together, and that here and now.* We all agree that until Christ came all the people of the world were divided into two groups:

1. Those in rebellion against God.
2. Those in the dispensation of the Father.

Then a new dispensation was vouchsafed to the world, and this, the dispensation of the Son, made possible for man wider religious horizons and deeper religious experiences. However, it will be found from the New Testament story that those in the dispensation of the Son constituted only a small group. The inauguration of the dispensation of the Son was followed in less than four years by the inauguration of the dispensation of the Holy Spirit. At that time the number in the dispensation of the Holy Spirit was also small, and too, though the numbers steadily increased, those two groups have remained small to this day in proportion to the first two groups noted above. In this country in our evangelistic churches the test has often been made of the spiritual condition of the assembled congregation, and usually only a small proportion of the people will testify by standing that they are conscious of sins forgiven, and of their acceptance with God. A much smaller number, if any at all, will testify to the experience variously called sanctification, Christian perfection, victorious living, or the baptism of the Holy Ghost. Now let us consider the situation more fully. Jesus made possible for all people a wonderful religious experience. Soon after, the Holy Spirit was given in great power, an experience so powerful that those entering into it were astounded at the graciousness of it, and the evidence of it amazed the onlookers. And yet after nearly two thousand years the great mass of the peoples of the world do not have experimental knowledge of either of these experiences. Though this is true, it is nevertheless true that those who have received these great blessings have exerted a profound influence upon their fellows, both directly and indirectly.

But why is the number so small who have received these larger and fuller experiences? One answer may be "everything worth while costs, and most people have not been willing to pay the price." Others have been lacking in knowledge or faith. This may be better understood by a historic review of the last 1900 years.

A RELIGIOUS RETROSPECT

A Religious Retrospect

Christianity beginning at Jerusalem spread out rapidly after Pentecost. Persecutions were frequent, but instead of checking it, they hastened its extension into the surrounding countries. Samaria, Antioch, Alexandria, Ephesus, and other important centers were soon reached by devoted Christians. Then Paul encouraged and directed by a vision to do so, went over into Europe, and henceforth that continent was to be the great religious battleground of the world. Philippi, Corinth, Constantinople, Rome, France, Spain, Britain, and contiguous lands were reached and evangelzed.

There was scarcely any part of the far-flung Roman Empire, either city or country, where gospel preachers had not gone. The gospel they preached was that which the Apostles had preached. In view of the fact that Paul's extensive missionary journeys, numerous letters to the churches, and his clear and forceful reasoning, it is easy to see that his teaching and influence would be very powerful. Only less would be that of John, who lived to be very old, and who, because of his intimate association with, and his knowledge of Jesus, together with his own notably holy life, had an exalted place among his fellows. Peter, too, because of the aggressiveness of his nature, his devotion to his Lord, and his genius for leadership, also left his impress upon the early church. The deity of Jesus was the central theme of all these, and indeed of all the early preachers.

To a world worn and weary, and sick at heart, it was a joyous message that God had come to earth, that He actually loved men; that He indeed loved them so much that He was willing to die for them, and did; that the grave could not hold Him; that He broke the bonds of the tomb, and that He lives now and forever.

But early in the fourth century persecutions had ceased, and Christianity had many members of wealth, learning, and power, including the Emperor Constantine, who in 311 threw the full influence of the empire to the Church. Now it would seem that the growth of the Church would be phenomenal. And so it was. But with this there came a terribly discordant note.

ARIANISM

Arius, a preacher of Alexandria, Egypt, alleged that it was impossible for the human mind to accept the belief that Jesus was God. Arius was very eloquent and vigorous, and he soon had a large following. He was very earnestly opposed by a brilliant young preacher named Athanasius. It was essentially a conflict of rationalism against the supernatural. The conflict with varying degrees of intensity raged throughout almost the entire fourth century to the great hurt of the Church. But Arianism lost out, and the Church again accepted without question the belief in the deity of Jesus.

This was the first of three similar conflicts in which the whole Church has been affected, the other two being deism in the eighteenth century, and modernism in the twentieth.

During the first three centuries with periodic persecutions the Church was notably pure. But now it enters a period when corruption began to be more and more evident. There were three special reasons for this:

1. Arianism, as just indicated.

2. The freedom from persecution, and the popularity of the Church after Constantine's acceptance of Christianity.

3. Great barbarian invasions.

In practically all the large cities there came to be great churches. The ministers of those churches were prominent and influential. Much more so were the bishops who had supervision over large districts. Because Rome was a great city and capital of the Empire, the bishop of that city and section came to be held in especially high esteem. Gradually claims were made for him that he had a higher authority than others, and finally, that he was preeminently the father, papa, or pope, of the entire Church, with powers not only greater than any others in the Church, but also greater than those of kings and emperors, and also with special spiritual power.

Christianity being always a missionary Church, they continued sending missionaries to other sections and countries. But now a new element changed the situation greatly. Great hordes of barbarians—Goths, Huns, Vandals, Franks, and others from the northeast—began to pour into southern and western Europe. They were rough and coarse, but virile. They appropriated what they wanted of the highest civilization known. Rome was captured by them in 476.

Before this the Roman Empire for a better administration had been divided into a western division with Rome as capital, and an eastern division with Constantinople as Capital. The Eastern Empire did not fall at this time, but remained a great power until it fell before the Turks in 1453. The civil government and the Church had been so closely identified that a separation in the church, too, seemed inevitable. Also a good many differences had developed. The greatest was that the eastern sections did not recognize the authority of the pope, and thus escaped many of the corruptions that were inherent in that unscriptural assumption of authority. On the other hand the Eastern division was much more closely aligned with the civil government, and there were corruptions in that connection which the western section largely escaped because there were no strong nations in the west for some centuries. Then there were intellectual differences, representative of the two sections. The two sections gradually drifted apart, and the final separation took place about the year 882. However, it may be noted that the religious conditions of the two were and are very similar, the east probably being better except in Russia. There the relationship of Church and State was close and both became very corrupt. The disreputable collapse of both was one of the tragedies of the first world war days. We can only hope that the masses of the people have in them the fundamentals of the gospel, and that these may indeed prove to be sources of great spiritual power in the days and years that are ahead.

Following the fall of Rome in 476 there was a period of about a thousand years often spoken of as the dark ages. They were not altogether dark, but they were rough and coarse, and also dark in the sense that they lacked the brilliance of Athens and Rome in the days of their glory on the one hand, and the greater glories of the western nations in recent centuries. In reality it was a very important period, but may be called the budding rather than the flowering and fruiting of our modern civilization.

The general effect of the barbarian invasion was that the barbarians became members of the Christian Church, and the spiritual level of their lives was raised. But they carried a good deal of their heathenism with them into the Church, and the spiritual tone of the Church was lowered. The resulting Church was really a blending of Christianity and heathenism.

THE FEUDAL SYSTEM

The nations that were later to become great were as yet simply in process of formation. To prevent utter chaos and anarchy something else was needed. This was evolved in what came to be known as the feudal system. In this system a large number of weak men joined themselves to a strong man, and they together formed a unit for mutual protection from enemies, and for mutual cooperation for sustenance. This system had often for its center a big, uncomfortable brick or stone structure or castle in which the big man lived, and to which the weaker ones could come in time of danger, and from which they would go out when necessary to war. The head of this group together with many others of the same sort were members of another group with a still stronger man over them. And this extended through various graduations up to Emperor. It was never an ideal system but because of the military and economic needs of the time it served for a long period a noble purpose.

During all this period the Church played a great and most beneficent part. Besides furnishing the comforts of religion and the peace of heart that no earthly source could give, it was distinctively a defender and protector of the poor and needy. While credit for much of this was due to the regular Church organization, a large part was due to another agency.

MONASTICISM

Among the more thoughtful men among heathen peoples there are three opinions that can usually be noted, and this in spite of the crude ignorance and superstition of the masses of the people. These are: 1st, a belief in a supreme higher power; 2nd, a consciousness of sin; 3rd, a need for the expiation of sin. The method for this expiation constitutes the most outstanding difference between Christianity and heathenism. Christ's way, however difficult for Himself, for the sinner is both simple and satisfying. It is simply faith in Jesus Christ. But the way of heathenism is in theory complex and in practice heartbreaking. According to them the flesh is corrupt and corrupting, and the only way to attain saintliness is in crucifying it. Their efforts to do this have often been very pathetic. During the medieval period, because of the unfaithfulness of so many of the leaders of the Christian Church, the simple method of Jesus was largely lost sight of, and the heathen method of bodily affliction had taken its place. The time came when numbers of earnest men burdened with a sense of sin sought relief through the heathen method. Among the means employed were: refraining from marriage; having but little food and that of the poorest quality; having but little protection from the heat of summer or the cold of winter; living apart from others as much as possible; sometimes spending their time in coves in the mountains or in huts in the edge of the desert, thus giving themselves to prayer and meditation; subjecting their bodies to painful flagellation and laceration. It seems strange to us that they so completely overlooked the fact that however isolated they were they could not rid themselves of their riotous imagination. Extremists in self-infliction have often been the subjects of mirth, but in reality they were deserving of the sincerest pity.

When such cases had multiplied until they were quite large it occurred to some thoughtful men to arrange for a large building where many could live together. They would live under the same hard conditions as before and be separate and apart from the world, and even live apart from each other except to have long and wearisome song and devotional services together. In some cases they were not even allowed to talk during meals. In order to join they had to take very strict vows of poverty, chastity, and obedience to superiors. It was a hard and unnatural existence. In all this there was no concern for others—for the home folks left behind, for the hungry, sick or distressed about them. It was simply an effort to get rid of their own sins. This attitude was thoroughly unchristian, for Jesus went about doing good.

But now a new element was added, a Christian ele-

ment—service. Some able and devout leaders, using
the above ideas as a base built a great superstructure
of institutional monasticism that affected directly or indirectly practically all the people of Europe. There
were several large orders and a vast number of monasteries differing more or less, but they were all funda-
mentally alike. This new Christian element of service
was the particular feature of monasticism that made it
the tremendous power it became during much of the
medieval period. Because of the admixture of Christianity and heathenism some of their activities were
helpful and some hurtful. Their useful services included quite a variety of duties: They went out as
preachers and missionaries; they fed the hungry;
nursed the sick; protected the weak and innocent from
the strong and cruel. At a time when the masses of the
people were ignorant they kept alive intellectual fires.
Among them were scholars who before the days of
printing wrote out by hand many Bibles and other
books. This is to say, they were the publishing houses
of their time. They also did considerable teaching. We
owe them a vast debt of gratitude for their service in
these fields. They usually had adjoining the monasteries farm lands which they cultivated for food for
themselves, and often brought to the work an intelligence superior to that of the neighboring peasants, and
so helped farming conditions. There was another service they rendered that is seldom mentioned, but is
very worthwhile. They were friendly. They mingled
freely with people who needed friends, but had few,
and their sunshiny presence helped in the struggle of
life. Then, too, in that turbulent age they protected

those who sought protection from oppressors. They
were democratic. They were open to rich and poor,
and both alike were subject to the same severe regula-
tions. It was about the only chance a poor and unprivileged boy had of developing unusual gifts bestowed
upon him by God. Twenty-eight members of the
Benedictines have been made popes, many of them
having come from homes of poverty and ignorance.
While the individual monks were poor, some of their
monasteries came to be wealthy from gifts for endowment just as our modern colleges are endowed. This
extensive service brought many and large gifts until
they became very wealthy, owning at one time a third
of the land of Europe.

Nunneries were also established in which women
went who devoted their lives to religious work. They
rendered the kinds of service for which they were
peculiarly qualified, especially caring for the sick and
needy.

CORRUPTION IN THE CHURCH

It would be a most happy thing if we could stop
here. But we cannot. It is necessary for a clear understanding of the period to note that while there were
many good men and women in the Church, there were
also many who were self-seeking and corrupt. There
were in the Church many places of power and prestige.
Such places corrupt men sought and, in all too many
cases , secured. They used the power and wealth thus
secured not for the good of the people, but for their own
aggrandizement.

The sorrowful side of the Catholic Church may be

seen in three aspects, all closely related:

1. Corrupt leadership. The position of pope, cardinal, bishop, and other high positions were very remunerative, and came to be shamelessly bought and sold. Although priests were not permitted to marry, for generations it was not at all unusual for them to have mistresses. Many popes had children openly acknowledged in Rome. Some of them were made high officials in the Church, even as children, and received large incomes from their positions. Many of the monasteries, as indicated above, became very wealthy. With the wealth there came self-indulgence on the part of the monks, and lax discipline on the part of the management. This continued until the corruption became so notorious that in one country after another they were regulated, suppressed or destroyed.

2. Corrupt doctrines. This was a natural resultant of a corrupt leadership. The great fundamental doctrines of Christianity were perverted to justify moral looseness, and to bring large revenues into the Church..

3. Persecutions. A system of persecutions was inaugurated that was meant to silence any criticism of Church beliefs and practices. Heresy-hunting became the first concern of great numbers, and heresy meant any activity, whether deed, word, thought or imagination against the Church organization. Starting with trials of individual critics, the movement soon extended to wide communities and nations. This came to be one of the principal objectives of the Society of Jesus, organized in 1534 by Ignatius Loyola. The Jesuits, as their members were called, accepted as a working prin-

ciple that the end justifies the means. That is, that
lying, stealing, immorality and even murder were justified if thereby the work of the Church might be pro-
moted. These persecutions reached their climax in the
inquisition in Spain. The human imagination was taxed
to contrive ever new and excruciating methods of affliction.

It may seem a small matter for a Church leader
here and there to become corrupt, but as these multiplied, and finally got control of the great central organization of the Vatican in Rome the harmful effects became world-wide. Now, after the lapse of centuries we
can get a view of the situation that reveals to us its
effects not only upon individuals and communities, but
upon nations. Spain at one time was the most powerful
country in the world, but she sold herself to do evil,
and today she has not only lost her power, and is one
of the weakest nations, but as a nation she has largely
lost the respect and esteem of the world. Later, France
was the greatest nation of the world. In 1572 in the
terrible massacre of St. Bartholomew's day 70,000
Huguenots, including most of the leaders, were mur-
dered. Following the revocation of the Edict of Nantes
in 1695 five hundred thousand fled the country. Many
of these were small manufacturers who had industrial
secrets of great actual and potential value. A large
proportion of these went to England, and there helped
to make England the greatest manufacturing country
in the world.

The next century a great struggle of world-wide influence took place between England and France for the
control of North America in the West, and of India in

the East. The struggle was hotly contested, and finally won, but not easily, by England. According to Thomas Carlyle, France just before St. Bartholomew's Day "was in a hair-breadth of becoming Protestant." It seems not unreasonable to believe that France's loss and England's gain during that period of persecution was sufficient to turn the tide in favor of England in those great sectors. Here we see how a few corrupt and scheming ecclesiastics and rulers probably changed the whole course of modern history.

Germany under the influence of Luther made a valiant start for a higher spiritual life—and it meant just that for multitudes. At the same time she began to make and for generations continued to make enormous strides in every line of material development. But pride of learning and individual and national ambition led them to forsake the Book that told them of the character and purposes of Luther's God, and the nation—as a nation—reverted to paganism. All this was done in Germany in its earlier stages in the name of religion, as had been the case though differently in France. To-day the condition of France is pathetic beyond the power of language to tell, and the condition of Germany is possibly even worse.

It should be added that the Reformation helped not only those who went out, but those who remained in the Catholic Church. The morals of the popes for years have been above reproach. However, no pope has apologized, at least publicly, for the scandalous record of previous popes. On the contrary the infallibility of the popes has been insisted on more in recent years than formerly. The morals of the priests in countries predominantly Protestant have also been generally good. The reports from countries predominantly Catholic have not been so favorable.

With the mingling of good and evil in the Catholic Church there has been one especially encouraging note. It has kept as the foundation of its faith, however encrusted with error, the three great facts of Christ: 1st, His supernatural birth; 2nd, His sacrificial death; and 3rd, His glorious resurrection.

The supernatural birth and the resurrection of Jesus are of great importance as aids to our faith. But the sacrificial death of Jesus is the greatest fact in all the universe. The following conversation between two thoughtful men may make the matter clearer:

Question: "Every transgression of a physical law meets penalty, does it not?"

Answer: "Yes."

Question: "There is no pardon, then, for such transgressions?"

Answer: "No."

Question: "Is there a radical difference between transgression of physical and transgressions of moral laws?"

Answer: "No. I suppose not."

Question: "Well, then, if God pardons the transgression of moral laws what becomes of the penalty?"

The doctors of the world testify that punishment for the transgression of physical laws is inexorable. What is the situation as to the punishment for the transgression of moral law? A heartbroken world testifies both as to the number and awfulness of the moral transgressions and the suffering resulting therefrom. Is there a remedy, is there a way by which the spiritual life may be regenerated and the suffering escaped, or must the world go down engulfed in its own moral rottenness? Thank God, there is a remedy. Untold millions of the best people throughout the ages bear glad testimony to this truth and with them it has not been simply a theory but a deep personal experience. How was it done? No philosopher or scientist has ever even suggested how this can be done. But the Bible, the only original source book on the subject is, in its entirety, centered about that one thought.

Leaving out all theories the answer is simple. It was by the sacrificial death of Jesus Christ. "The blood of Jesus Christ, His Son, cleanseth us from all sin."

It is the glory of the Catholic Church that in spite of all its errors and corruption it has never lost sight of this great central truth. There have been many times when it seemed almost submerged, but the efficacy of the cross though often ignored has never been officially denied. But just here Protestantism is facing its greatest danger. The cross is an offense to modernism, and a distressingly large number of preachers consider themselves and their congregations entirely too refined for a gospel of blood.

In America during all our early history the Catholic Church as a minority group quietly accepted the role. But in recent years there has been a marked change in its attitude. In Europe, hitherto their stronghold, the Catholics have suffered greatly in physical and material things, but what is even more serious their ideology has been hit hard in nearly every country. But in America in addition to material prosperity there has been notable progress in practically all their activities. This has emboldened them to ask or demand many privileges and advantages not previously considered possible for them, from local, state and federal government.

At the same time that they are seeking special favors for themselves in this country, they are using every device to get our government to prevent our missionaries from going into the Catholic countries to the south of us, although our missionaries are receiving a warm welcome from many of the leaders of those countries.

Their numbers and interest have notably increased in recent years, and have reached an all time high mark, their numbers being greater than the largest Protestant denomination, and in many of our largest cities they have greater political power than all of Protestantism together. This, too, at a time when nearly all the Protestant denominations have seen a decline. The Sunday school attendance of most Protestant denominations has been decreasing for several years. General moral laxness had become serious before the outbreak of the war, and worse since.

This situation has very naturally been disturbing to well-informed Protestants. Not a few remedies have been suggested, but generally they have been simply palliatives. There is one remedy—and only one—for this distressing situation. That remedy is the preaching from burning hearts of salvation from sin through the blood of Jesus Christ. That modernism does not and cannot do. We are therefore brought face to face with the fact that modernism cannot meet the needs of our time. It has been tried and found wanting. We simply must return to the faith of our fathers, if we would escape from a terrible collapse of our attainments and ideals.

THE JEWS

As the warm waters of the gulf stream flow through the Atlantic Ocean so the Jewish people have flowed through the nations of the earth. This striking illustration by Senator Zebulon B. Vance gives in few words an epitome of Jewish history. Their racial solidarity in spite of the fact that they have no home of their own and are widely scattered among the nations, and in spite of almost constant persecutions, is nothing less than an ethnological miracle. In the early ages it was their religion, and the social isolation that it enforced, and their customs different from others that was the cause of the persecution. Many times, in the opinion of their enemies, they have been utterly annihilated. But from every conflict they have emerged with increased strength. Originally, mostly herdsmen and farmers and intense lovers of the land, the time came when the holding of real property was difficult or impossible because of unjust taxation or confiscation. They have been industrious and thrifty, and naturally created savings, and as naturally put them as a matter of safety into money and precious jewels. In this way they came to be the money lenders of Europe in the middle ages. They also showed a marked aptitude for trade, and with available money it was a natural outlet for their energies. But they became notorious for their sharp practices, and especially for charging usurious rates of interest. Their international connections enabled them to get money from prosperous sections to purchase distressed property in sections where local money was not available. In this way much serious friction resulted, and this in turn was the occasion of more persecutions.

While this situation was general there were many notable exceptions. The family of Rothchilds, for a long time the greatest bankers and the wealthiest family in the world, laid the basis of their great business and wealth by dealings of strict honesty, and by an unusual fidelity to an important trust. In recent centuries the Jews have rendered notable service in the professions, especially in music, literature, and medicine.

The Jews have in the past been persecuted by the Greek Church, the Catholic Church and the Protestants. But in our own time there has been in one respect a gratifying change. Catholics and Protestants have united in their earnest and vigorous protests against their persecution by Hitler and others like-minded. No other race has for so long a period and throughout such wide territory played such an important part as have the Jews. And the end is not yet. From the teachings of the Bible and of history we have good reason to believe that they will continue to be a mighty factor in the affairs of the world.

THE HOLY ROMAN EMPIRE

Charlemagne, the greatest ruler of the middle ages, established the Holy Roman Empire and was crowned emperor of it by the pope in the year 800. His territory included the present countries of France, Germany,

Austria, Belgium, Switzerland, Hungary, and parts of Spain and Italy, and in theory it was a re-establishment of the Western Roman Empire which had fallen in 476. After Charlemagne's death the empire was divided among his three sons, forming the basis of the three modern nations of France, Germany, and Italy. In its foundation both Church and State participated, and this fact was the occasion for a more or less constant struggle between the popes and the civil authorities of Germany for nearly a thousand years. It was finally put out of commission by Napoleon in 1806.

Our present interest in this is that whether for good or for evil one far-reaching result was that it delayed until the latter part of the 19th century the formation of strong national governments in Germany and Italy. Because of this, while the other governments of Western Europe were securing great sections of territory in America, Asia and Africa these two nations were left out. The determination of Germany, and to a less extent of Italy, to get what they considered their share was one of the main causes of the two world wars. Their main contention was for part of Africa, but Germany went far beyond that in her mad ambition to make all central Europe and beyond contributory to her.

<h3 style="text-align:center">MOHAMMED</h3>

In the meantime a new element arose that was to affect every phase of life for many centuries. In the seventh century in Arabia there arose a man by the name of Mohammed who claimed to be a great prophet, and who was the founder of a new religion. He had come into slight contact with Jews and Christians. He wrote a book called the Koran, which he claimed to be divinely inspired, and which he gave to his followers as their Bible. His purpose seems to have been sincere and earnest. He taught that there was one God, and that Mohammed was his prophet. This, at least, was probably better than the worship of many Gods, which had before this been their custom. But for the first several years he had only slight success. Then certain circumstances caused him to take the sword, and with notable success. It is not difficult to believe that Satan offered him the kingdoms of the world if he would worship him, and that he accepted that proposition. At any rate, his followers took the sword, and thus began a series of military victories that continued off and on for centuries. Beginning in Arabia they went on until they became masters of Western Asia, Northern Africa and parts of Southern Europe. The situation looked ominous for Christendom. In addition to the fact that the Arabs were of a militant disposition, they were encouraged further by the promise of valuable loot from conquered cities and countries, and also by the assurance that if they died fighting for their religion they would be sure of heaven where there would be unnumbered beautiful women for their enjoyment. They were finally checked by Charles Martel at the battle of Tours, France, in 732. While their expansion was checked, their influence has continued to affect the world in many different ways.

THE CRUSADES

The most notable and direct way was the Crusades.

The Mohammedans, originally Arabs, but later also Turks, or infidels, as the Christians called them, had taken early in their career the Holy Land, and thus held Jerusalem and all the places most dear to the followers of Jesus. The opinion was expressed that the Christians should recover this land from the infidels. The suggestion had a most remarkable response, and all over Southern and Central and Western Europe groups were formed for this purpose. They united into masses large enough to be called armies, but were poorly organized and equipped. Wave after wave of them went out through a period of about 200 years. A great deal of heroism and sacrifice was manifested, but not much judgment. They had some military successes, but never did succeed in their real purpose of securing permanently the Holy Land. Even today while the Holy Land was entrusted to Great Britain as a mandate after the First World War the Mohammedans and Jews are in bitter conflict for supremacy. But the Crusades did render a valuable service in checking the Moslem advance.

The Crusades had other far-reaching effects, both for good and for evil. I will mention one of them.

Reference has been made to the fact that the Mohammedans promised heaven to those who died fighting. The Christians had already become so corrupt in doctrine that they did not hesitate to promise their warriors the same privilege—heaven while fighting or on a crusade for the Lord. Not only was this true, but it led to worse corruptions. If a man's sins could be remitted for fighting for a righteous cause, they might be remitted for other meritorious deeds; and finally for a cash contribution. Thus the flood-gates of corruption were opened up, getting worse and worse until checked by Luther.

THE CRIMEAN WAR, A CRUSADE OF THE   GREEK CHURCH

While the Catholic Church was pouring itself out lavishly in the Crusades the Greek Church held aloof, and in some cases was hostile because of the bad behavior of some of the Crusaders. But the time came when it too entered into a somewhat similar struggle, though in a very different way. The Patriarch, the head of the Greek Church, lived in Constantinople, as that important city was the headquarters of that Church, just as Rome was of the Catholic Church. When the Mohammedan Turks in 1453 captured Constantinople and surrounding country it was a serious and humiliating blow to the Church. The Russian people, including her rulers, were bigoted adherents of that Church, and this was particularly humiliating to them inasmuch as Russia was by this time a more powerful country than Turkey. So it seemed the natural thing for Russia to take over the city and surrounding country. There was another big reason why Russia wanted and needed Constantinople. Although Russia was a vast country with a very large population and immense natural resources she had no year-round access to the sea. Her ports on the Baltic were ice-bound for several months each year. She wanted Constantinople so that her war and merchant vessels might in this way have access to the Mediterranean Sea, and out to the world.

The longing for Constantinople on the part of Russia

has been one of the biggest factors in European politics for more than three hundred years. If she was stronger than Turkey, why did she not just go in and take it? The other nations of Europe prevented it. It was certainly not because of any fondness for Turkey on the part of the leading European countries, for her government was perhaps the worst in the world, and her people were notoriously cruel and bloodthirsty—and this has been true until this present generation when there has been a very great improvement in people and government. But Russia did not take Constantinople because the great European governments were afraid to let Russia become too powerful, and so they blocked any movement in that direction for many years.

However, in 1853 the matter came to an issue largely because of the selfishness and vanity of Louis Napoleon, Emperor of France, and Nicholas, Czar of Russia. Constantinople was almost as sacred to the Russians as Jerusalem was to the Catholics, and the capture of that holy city from the infidel Mohammedans was urged by the Russian Government with every possible means of propaganda, especially through the churches. The result was that Russia became aflame with religious fanaticism. The Crimean War was the result. Nicholas had convinced himself that England would not enter the war against him, and consequently was greatly surprised and disappointed when she did so. The war was badly managed on both sides and the casualties were estimated at five millions, the loss from famine and pestilence being greater than from the sword. But Russia did not get Constantinople, nor has she since. But the longing for it is still in every Russian breast, and no plans for the future of Europe can ignore it.

THE RENAISSANCE

The capture of Constantinople and surrounding country in 1453 by the Turks also had far-reaching effects in Southern and Western Europe. In that city and section there were many scholarly men and much culture. The conditions were made so severe for them that large numbers went to the countries of Western Europe, and many of them became teachers. For more than two centuries the intellectual situation had been improving. And now a great impetus was given to it, and the Renaissance was the result. It was a mighty intellectual awakening. We are here not interested so much in the Renaissance as such, but because it helped to pave the way for the Reformation.

The corruption of the Church about which several references have already been made had become so brazenly open, and all the high-ups in the Church seemed so tolerant of it, and even participating in its loot, that it seemed foolhardy for anybody to undertake to do anything about it. John Huss and many others had lost their lives trying to improve conditions. Why attempt the impossible.

But a new day was dawning. Men's minds were opening. It would seem that Martin Luther was raised up for such a time as this. There might be a chance now.

MARTIN LUTHER AND THE REFORMATION

When men begin obeying God they never know how zigzag the way may be, nor what the end will be like.

They know only one thing, that they will have glorious companionship on the way, even His own presence.

Conditions in Luther's home city in Germany had become almost unbelievably bad. The Church organization would seemingly do anything to get money. The plan now being vigorously and enthusiastically used was in charge of a man named Tetzel who was working under the direction of some higher-ups. He made a strong box and made a hole in it big enough for silver coins. For so much money the poor people might pay their loved ones out of a burning purgatory. And their souls would fly out of purgatory as soon as the money hit the bottom of the box. Then, too, they could for so much money assure themselves of safety from a burning hell. And so the poor, ignorant people flocked to him and put in their money, and the coffers of the Church, and of some individuals who manipulated it, bulged with the ill- gotten accumulations.

Martin Luther, a scholar, a teacher, a religious leader, protested. He did not realize how deeply entrenched the evil was. If he had known he would no doubt have acted as he did anyway. It was a terrific struggle. His life was in danger for long periods at a time. But his work was not yet finished, and God raised up friends and protection. The corruption was manifested in many ways. But the heart of the struggle that Luther had was between faith and works. The Church had gradually built up a system of salvation by works. Say so many prayers, do so much religious work, make a pilgrimage, fight in a battle for God, and especially pay so much money to the Church, and as a result salvation now and forever would result. But Luther had learned from the Bible that "the just shall live by faith." He had been very slow in learning it, and had suffered much in his own life before learning it. Now he tells others about it. The leaders did not want such preaching because if the common people should come to believe it their living would be affected. That hell and purgatory be made to appear as severe as possible, and a way provided to escape it by paying money into the Church was a profitable scheme, and they did not want it interferred with.

No doubt great numbers of the more intelligent and devout were troubled about the situation, but seemed helpless even to undertake to improve conditions. But now with great teachers speaking out, and the minds of men opening up in the new tonic atmosphere of the Renaissance, the time seemed ripe for a cleansing of the Church.

It is to be expected but marvelous nevertheless that when God lays upon a man a difficult but important task He always selects one who is peculiarly fitted for it. So it was here. Martin Luther by natural ability, training, and experience was the man for the heart-breaking task.

But one naturally wonders how the Church could ever get in such a condition. The answer must be that it came about so gradually that the successive generations became accustomed to it. Then, too, it is easy to believe what one learns at his mother's knee. It came to be the belief and teaching of the Church that one could do more than was required, this being especially true of martyrs, and this accumulation of extra good works together with the inexhaustible treasure of the merits of Christ could be used by the Church to relieve men of the penalty of their sins, this being done generally at a price somewhat in accordance with their abilitly to pay. The pope who claimed to be the vice-regent of Christ claimed to have these merits at his disposal. In addition to this larger treasury anyone, a priest, for instance, might say more prayers or do more work than it was necessary for him to do, and could use this extra accumulation to help someone who was behind with his praying, or who was living such a life that the quality of his prayers was defective. Incidentally, most of the praying was not to Jesus, but to the mother of Jesus and to certain saints of the past as intermediaries on the supposition that they would be more approachable.

PURGATORY AND THE INTERMEDIATE STATE

Purgatory was a corruption of one of the great beliefs of the early Church, viz., the intermediate state. The corruption here was so great that it became the very center of the battle between the organized Church and the reformers. It had come to be one of the greatest sources of revenue for the Church, and a great many influential men in the organization participated in the ill-gotten gains. So intense was their opposition to the evils of purgatory that the reformers in fighting this corruption almost entirely overlooked its sound foundation—the intermediate state. The result has been that this has been the great neglected doctrine of the Church; while a belief in it has not quite been considered heresy, it has at least been regarded as a very questionable doctrine. When Dr. (later, Bishop) H. N.

McTyeire, one of the most profound and influential preachers our country has produced, some eighty years ago preached an able sermon favoring the belief it was so unusual as to cause very extensive comment. In view of this situation a brief review of the subject should be made.

It may be said in general that the practice of the Catholic Church was not to create new and false doctrines but to corrupt sound ones, and the very fact of a corrupt doctrine of purgatory is strongly indicative of a pure and unadulterated foundation from which the corruption sprang. The scriptural foundation is to the effect that between death and the general resurrection the souls of the departed go into the spirit world, the good into a better condition, the bad into a worse, and that between them is a great gulf fixed so that no one can go from one to the other. Hades is the Greek word for this spirit world. This word is generally translated hell in the King James version. In the revised versions it has been changed. Gehenna is the word used for the final place of the lost. Hades includes both the good and the bad. For the good division other names are given, as Paradise, Abraham's bosom, etc. No special name is given for that side of the gulf in which the wicked are placed.

Jesus said to the thief on the cross, "This day shalt thou be with me in Paradise." After three days, on the morning of the resurrection He said to Mary, "Touch me not for I have not yet ascended unto my Father." It would seem that during these three days He had not been in heaven but in Paradise. There are a number of other passages of a similar sort.

The doctrine of the intermediate state is strongly re-inforced by the belief and preaching of the early leaders of the Christian Church: It was the belief of Justin Martyr, A. D. 150; Irenæus, A. D. 180; Tertullian, A. D. 200; Clement born about 50 years after the death of St. John, and his great disciple, Origen; Chrysostom and Athanasius A. D. 350-400, just to mention a few of the most prominent. These were all able and vigorous exponents of this doctrine. Of the great modern religious leaders none has been more emphatic than Mr. Wesley. In a sermon on Dives and Lazarus he says: "It is very generally supposed that the souls of good men, as soon as they are discharged from the body go directly to heaven; but this opinion does not have the least foundation in the oracles of God . . . Paradise is not heaven. It is indeed (if I may be allowed the expression) the ante-chamber (elsewhere 'porch') of heaven."

The purgatory of the Catholic Church offered a second chance. That belief grew up rather gradually. The reformers and practically all modern preachers felt that this was unscriptural and but an encouragement of and conducive to careless living in this world. For their opposition the reformers had strong scriptural proof. Paul said, "We must all appear before the judgment seat of Christ, that everyone may receive the things done in the body, according to that he hath done whether it be good or bad." *The things done in the body* are to form the basis of judgment. Then, too, the importance of turning to God in this life is the insistent note in all Biblical teachings. But perhaps the most serious corruption was that in this period pardon could be purchased by loved ones on earth with money.   The work of reformers in fighting this evil was so successful that as a belief and practice it was entirely eliminated from the Protestant Churches, and its evils greatly lessened in the Catholic Church.

But there is another phase of the intermediate state that is of interest, viz., what occurs during that period. How do the souls of those who have gotten into this Paradise spend their time?   We need here reverent reticence.   The Scriptures have not spoken explicitly. There should be no vain or irreverent curiosity.   However, if there are great truths that are consonant with all the revealed truth that we have—truths that may bring help and encouragement to many, we do not want carelessly to neglect them.   In a later chapter it is brought out that the determining factor in our destiny is attitude.   If our attitude is one of obedience and reverence we will be enrolled with those who love the Lord, but if our attitude is one of rebellion against God that fact separates us from Him.   But among those whose attitude is such as will enable them to enter paradise there is a very wide range, including the saint at the top, and at the bottom one perhaps who never even heard the name of Jesus, but who has endeavored to be true to the highest and the best that he knew. There are four particulars in which all those in paradise are alike:

1.   They are all going in the same direction; they all have their faces turned Godward.

2.   They are free from the weaknesses of the flesh, for they have left their physical bodies behind.

3.   Satan is shut out from them; he is on the other

side of the great gulf, or on earth.

4. They are also free from the influence of evil men —those who would purposely or indifferently lead them astray.

But there is a vast difference in knowledge, consecration and faith. Are we presumptuous if we accept the belief that those who are richly endowed in this respect may help those who for any reason are weak and ignorant? And we must believe there are many such unless we accept the belief that death works a transformation. That such a transformation is affected by death we have no scriptural or other evidence. Indeed, all the evidence we have is to the contrary. We carry with us the character that we have wrought out here.

One of the distinctive characteristics of a saint here is a disposition to help others in any way possible. Can we think then that on the other side he would refuse to help someone not so richly endowed as he; indeed can we imagine that he could restrain himself from such service? Therefore, I do not think that we are doing violence to the Scriptures when we assume that there will be great helpful cooperation in that transition period. It may be compared to a beautiful family life in which the little children are given by wise and loving parents instruction and discipline for their enjoyment of a fuller life and more efficient service in future years. It may be that we all may thus acquire the fitness needed to occupy the mansions Jesus has gone on to prepare for us.

In this connection may we not consider one of the most perplexing doctrines of our religion, viz., elec-

tion or predestination. There was a time when a large
proportion of Protestants believed and taught that certain people were elected or predestined to be saved, and
that therefore they would be saved regardless of whatever they might do. As only those so elected could be
saved it was inevitable that all others would be lost,
regardless of anything that they might do. A sense of
the unfairness and injustice of such a doctrine rankled
in the hearts of many, and finally when Wesleyan and
Methodist preachers proclaimed the consoling truth
that whosoever will may be saved, this terrible interpretation had to yield to saner views.

However, the doctrine of predestination remains. It
is taught in the Bible with a positiveness that cannot be
denied, and St. Paul evidently considered it an important and precious doctrine. But to this day there has
been no interpretation that has received general acceptance. The feeling is general that it is one of the great
truths that we may not be able to understand till we
cross over to the other side.

But there are those who believe that here we have
a true and satisfying solution of the admittedly difficult
passages on this subject. In a later chapter there is discussed the question as to who will have the blessed
privilege of being forever with his Lord, and who will
forever be cast from His presence. That this will be
determined not by verbal professions but by attitude is
in accordance with the teachings of Jesus. Granting
this, it seems reasonable to believe that vast multitudes
—even many billions—who have lived through successive generations, may have such an attitude that they
may enter paradise. But it seems reasonable, too, to

believe that many of them—most of them in fact—will have but slight knowledge of God, and varying degrees of faith and consecration. It has seemed to pious and thoughtful minds that though these did not have the rebellious attitude that would make it necessary for them to be shut out from God and cast into hell, neither were they prepared to enter at once into the glories of heaven. Do we not have reason to believe that those who have an attitude of obedience and reverence to God, though very immature, may be placed on one side of the great gulf fixed, and those in positive rebellion against God on the other? Most of these on the Paradise side we may reasonably believe are immature spirits who have had but little spiritual instruction or help in this world.

In many cases it has been through no fault of their own. Reverent students of the character of God feel that it is not at all like Him to cut them off without giving them every chance possible. And in this period before the judgment is there not good reason to believe that there is possible such a chance? Would it not be like God to furnish them the instruction and training needed for their greater happiness and usefulness? And, too, would it not be like God to plan for all this from the beginning, that is, to predestinate it? He could foresee a great need of teachers and leaders for this enormous task. In His infinite wisdom would He not from the beginning do whatever would be necessary to provide them?

We know that God's method is for some of God's children to help others. But one must have before he can give, whether of goods, knowledge, power or influence. God foreordained that certain ones should have special privileges not for themselves alone but also for the good of others. So it was with Abraham and with Isaiah and Paul, so it is with many a preacher today who is granted many spiritual privileges, but not for himself alone, but seemingly almost altogether for others. The Jews were so favored in spite of much unworthiness, because all the people of the world could best be helped in this way. The English speaking people have been marvelously blessed. May we not reverently ask if we with all our sins and weaknesses have not been predestined for such a time as this?

There can be no charge of favoritism in all this. Privilege there is, but service, not privilege, is the key word. In this service, if we interpret the Scriptures aright, Jesus set the example. In I Peter 3:19, 20, we are told that "in the spirit he went and preached unto the spirits in prison; which sometimes were disobedient when once the longsuffering of God waited in the days of Noah, while the ark was a preparing, wherein a few, that is, eight souls were saved by water." As His disciples have followed in His footsteps in preaching in this world, it may be that they will also follow His footsteps in preaching to those in the intermediate state who are immature but not rebellious. And may this not continue until the judgment when we will have an abundant entrance into our everlasting home?

Then, too, in the parable of the pounds he who shall here make the best possible use of the pound delivered to him is to rule over ten cities; and another who has made a good record is to rule over five cities. Is this simply pretty imagery, or is there a basis of reality in

it? Is it true that the man who in this world controlled
his own spirit and who lived so close to Christ that he
learned His secrets and caught His spirit will have the
privilege and responsibility of the oversight and training of others? Jesus on earth was orderly. When He
fed the 5,000 He had them to sit down by fifties on the
green grass. With the many billions in the intermediate state and the millions who have had special privileges on earth and have taken advantage of them, does
it not seem reasonable to think that there will be a marvelous organization, being in charge of those who know
Jesus best and love their fellows most.

And is it not a great incentive to faithful and heroic
living in this world if thereby we are fitting ourselves
not only for greater happiness but also nobler service
in the world to come.

HELL

Again, the teaching of the Catholic Church was that
the place of punishment was a place of actual physical
fire. That is to say that they took the words of Jesus
literally and not figuratively. The Protestants and reformers have gotten away from most of the hurtful beliefs which had accumulated in the Church. But this
last has lingered with the Protestant Church, and is
widely believed today. For that reason, it may be
desirable to discuss this matter a little more fully.

There are two outstanding figures in the New Testament describing the condition of the lost. There does
not always seem to be a clear differentiation in name as
to the punishment on the suffering side of the great
gulf in hades and that of the permanent place of pun-

ishment of the lost. It would seem that both are terrible beyond our imagination to conceive, but that the sufferings after the judgment will be in intensified form. To illustrate: On other pages is given some account of Frederick the Great, of Prussia. In his old age there were no physical needs unsupplied, but he was a very unhappy man—the thought of the miseries he had brought on others doubtless intensified the miseries of his own rebellious spirit. But the evil influences of his life did not cease at his death, but are continuing still. Even now in the global war his influence is being exerted more widely than ever before. The judgment pronounced at his death would not have been what it will be at the general judgment, and the consciousness of the continuing evils will press down upon him with increasing intensification. There is no indication anywhere that consciousness will in time or eternity cease to function, or that the burden of guilt will fall from the mind and heart of the troubled spirit. The two following figures are outstanding in any consideration of the condition of the lost:

First. Fire. Lake of fire. Furnace of fire. Gehenna of fire (Matt. 5:22 G'k). The Greek word gehenna is believed to have come from the word Hinnom. The Valley of Hinnom, a little way out of Jerusalem, was once a scene of horrible, idolatrous practices, and was on that account made a dumping ground for the garbage of the city. There the trash and the garbage of the city were taken. Fire was set to it and it smouldered and burned day and night, just as we see on the outskirts of our cities today. Things that were of use were not carried there, but worthless things, things that could not be used for the purpose for which they were made, and could not indeed serve any useful purpose. The thought seems to be clear that if we will not serve the purpose for which we were created, viz., to serve and worship God, then the inevitable thing is to be cast out from the habitations of men to be burned, just as the trash is burned.

Another figure that Christ used was the "outer darkness." A king made a great supper for the marriage of his son, but certain invited guests did not see fit to attend. He then sent out and gathered in all sorts of folks. Everything was free; bath, wedding robes, wedding feast. A group of clean, well-dressed, happy people was soon ready to enjoy the king's bounty. The king came in. What promised to be a most happy occasion was marred because one man was there in his filth and rags. He had such little respect for the king, such little appreciation of his kindness, he was so lazy and indifferent, so lacking in personal respect and decency that he would not take the little trouble necessary to bathe and dress. He did not belong to that group. It was simply inevitable that the king would have to put him out. So, while the others were enjoying the delicious meal provided by the king in a room where there was light and warmth and joy, this man was cast into the outer darkness. The point is plain. Our Father has prepared wonderful things for us. It is all without money and without price. It has truly been said that heaven is a prepared place for a prepared people. Those who refuse to prepare after everything has been so freely and graciously furnished cannot object if they are refused admittance into the goodly com-

pany. This makes it clear that those who are finally
cast out will be utterly speechless.

It seems perfectly plain that these are figures of
speech. Each one has a special significance.

As a young minister I was sent for one day to see a
sick man about an hour's drive from my study. He
was an old man of a once prominent family. But he
had used and sold whiskey and dope until he had come
to an utterly miserable condition. As I went into the
room he said, "Pray for me, pray for me, I am burning
up inside. If all the doctors of the city knew how I am
burning up, they would come to see me." I knelt and
tried to pray. He had yielded to unrighteous gratification of appetite and passion until he could get no relief.
A few months later he died in an insane asylum. This
figure and this illustration give some idea of the misery of those who give themselves up to a life of debauchery.

The figure of outer darkness may have special reference to those who hate or have no regard for their fellows, and are in rebellion against God. There are
those who are so filled with hate that it matters not how
delightful the outward conditions they themselves in
their inner life are in the outer darkness. Again, they
may think so much of money and the power it brings
that they lose a sense of the value of personality. They
are thoroughly selfish and avaricious. They are afraid
they will not get enough money or that they will lose
what they have. All they can see is the material. They
have no sure foundation, but are ever seeking one. They
have not learned that the only sure foundation is Jesus
Christ. Always afraid they will fall from their pedes-

tal and afraid of the pedestal itself, theirs is not a sure foundation but a foundation of sand. Having lost a sense of the personal worth of others they do not have fellowship with them and are therefore shut out. This may apply to the poor as well as the rich. For money in itself is not a curse, but the love of it, the trusting in it.

These are two of the most terrible figures possible for the human mind to grasp. But we may be sure the reality is worse than any description of it can be.

There is another thing about hell as we get the story in the case of the rich man and Lazarus. Note that the rich man in hades does not ask to get out; he begs for relief. That is true of the sinful life as we know it today. Here is a man given up to drink and dope and debauchery. He admits that he is miserable. We say to him, "Give your life to God, give up your evil companions." But he said, "No, I want more liquor, more dope, more evil companions." I saw on a glorious mountain side one beautiful Sabbath morning a man with a gun in his hands. The glories of the place and day were lost on him. He said a man had done him wrong, and he was going to kill him. I urged him to give up hate and yield himself to God. But not so, he wanted revenge.

We have seen men and women who had more money than they would ever need. They were unhappy because of losses, real or possible. We have urged them to use part of their money to enrich the lives of others. No, that was not what they thought they needed. What they wanted was more money.

There was another thing about the idea of hell

that was developed by the Catholic Church, and that has never been gotten rid of by the Protestants. Their teaching was that everyone would suffer alike, and that suffering in every case would be the worst conceivable. In my boyhood a young lady a few miles from my home went to a country, old-fashioned square dance, caught cold and pneumonia and died. The preacher who conducted the funeral stated brutally that she had gone to hell, and all his hearers knew that he meant a hell of literal fire. But Jesus told us that some would be beaten with many stripes, and others with few stripes.

HEAVEN

There have not been the differences of opinion about heaven as about hell. A few statements may be made on which there has been very general agreement by thoughtful students during the centuries since Christ came.

First, heaven is a place. There are substance and solidity in the idea. And it is a beautiful place. It may well be that much of the descriptions that are given in the Bible need to be understood figuratively, but there can be no doubt but that our glorified ears and eyes will be thoroughly pleased.

But most of us perhaps having borne the burdens of life and endured its sorrows will be more interested in the assurance that those things that bring distress will be forever shut out. No pain will be there nor sorrow nor crying. There will be no fear nor anxiety nor unsatisfied longings. But there will be a peace and a calm never to be disturbed.

There will be a reunion with our loved ones with

no fear of separation. In addition our circle of acquaintance with kindred spirits will be so enlarged that eternity will not be too long for the gladsome companionship. Best of all we shall have the privilege of personal association with our Lord.

Then, too, it has been the belief of many that the activities that we loved on earth but did not have the time, opportunity or ability to master may be carried on and perfected in the better land.

But no speculation is needed, because His word has revealed to us an assurance which is as a downy pillow for our weary head that when we awake with His righteousness we shall be *satisfied.*

Only a few of the corruptions in Martin Luther's day have been noted. I will mention just one other. In the Sacrament of the Lord's Supper, Jesus said, "This is my body. This is my blood." The Catholics had come to explain that this was to be literally and not figuratively understood. This and the ideas connected with it came to be very hurtful. But when we Protestants remember how easy and natural it has been for many of us from childhood to believe in a literal interpretation of the fire in hell we need all our charity when criticizing the Catholics for a literal interpretation of body and blood in the sacrament of the Lord's Supper.

It is interesting to note that Luther who became so outspoken against the corruptions of the Church, and who had as a priest married contrary to its teachings, could not get away altogether from this. He said that after the bread and wine were consecrated it was not really the body and blood of Christ, but that it was different from ordinary bread and wine. He gave as an illustration the fact that an iron poker put in the fire was still iron, but something was added—there was heat.

As the struggle developed and continued many other strong men came into prominence, as Erasmus, Melanchthon, Zwingli, Calvin, Knox, and others. While they differed in many ways, they all agreed on one thing, and that became the distinctive feature of the Reformation. They all agreed that the source of the truths to be accepted was the Bible, without ecclesiastical notes or priestly interpretation or mediation, and they stood unhesitatingly and unmovably upon it as their platform.

PRESBYTERIANS

John Calvin, founder of the Presbyterians, emphasized the greatness and majesty of God. No people ever get higher in character than the character of the God that they worship. John Knox in Scotland, believing in such a God, had such power in prayer that the worldly Mary, Queen of Scots, said she feared Knox's prayers more than an army. With this background it is very easy to understand how the Presbyterian Church has been such a tremendous power for righteousness through the world. It is also easy to understand how the people of little Scotland, eking out a bare physical existence on her rocky and sterile hills have furnished leaders for every great forward movement of modern times. However, in magnifyng the greatness of God there was danger of minimizing the greatness of man. Man is not a worm of the dust. He was made in the image and after the likeness of God. There were those who made that mistake. But saner views prevailed. They were saved from doctrinaire extremists by the waves of spiritual regeneration set in motion by John Wesley.

Calvinism was not democratic in origin or theory, but in practice it has been most effective in the development of the world's two greatest democracies. In England Cromwell with his Calvinistic round-heads gave autocracy a blow from which, despite some dying gasps, it never recovered. In America the Puritan and Separatist elements of New England and the Scotch-Irish of the Southern Piedmont—both largely Calvinistic—constituted the backbone of the Revolution, and in the formation and development of this great country they have continuously given intelligent and loyal cooperation.

EPISCOPALIANS

The Church of England and her daughter, the Protestant Episcopal Church in America, have been taunted with having an ignoble origin. That, however, is not justified by the facts. It is true that Henry VIII had the Catholic Church in England to free it from the Pope and the papal organization in Rome because the pope would not grant an unrighteous divorce that he wanted. But he was not the real founder of the Church of England. What he did was to make it possible. After his death the regents of his young son, Edward VI, put a group of noble and godly men in a responsible position in the Church, and these were the real founders of the Church. Weak and wicked men did not

write or edit the prayer book. Edward died after a
short reign of six years. His sister Mary, a bigoted
Catholic, then came to the throne, and she tried to undo
what had been done. But before getting it done she
died, and her sister, Elizabeth, became Queen. Elizabeth had many serious faults, but she made England a
great Queen. Whether from principle or political ex-
pediency, or both, she undid as expeditiously as possible the work of Mary, and carried forward the work as
planned by the religious leaders of Edward VI. During her long reign the foundations of the Church as we
have it were made secure.

BAPTISTS

The Baptist Church has been notable for two things.
The first everybody knows about. It has been strongly
and vigorously evangelical and evangelistic. Like the
Methodists it has gone out into the highways and by-
ways of life, and brought the multitudes into the kingdom. It has been stricter than any other of the larger
denominations in demanding a positive religious experience in those who seek for membership in the Church.
But it has rendered another great service to the Church
and the world that is not so familiar. It has fought per-
sistently and consistently against any union of Church
and State. Those who have had occasion or opportunity to know the evil effects of such unions in Europe can
appreciate the great privilege we enjoy in that respect
in America. The Baptists have stood during the years
and stand today as a rock wall against such union. The
other denominations have been glad to acknowledge
their supremacy in this field, and to follow their lead-

ership.

The Baptists have been democratic both in theory and practice, and their pervasive influence in almost every part of England and America has been most wholesome and far-reaching.

During the first seventeen centuries of the Christian era Asia was touched only on its western rim; Africa hardly at all; and the Americans only in the later period. The struggle of Christianity has been in Europe and for Europe. After Martin Luther's day Protestantism spread rapidly until those separating became comparable in number and power with those remaining in the Church, that is, in the northern countries. While many good people remained in the old Church and many not so good went with the Protestants it may be safely said that a very large proportion of the best and most aggressive people joined the Protestants.

THE THIRTY YEARS' WAR

With the cleavage there came a period of bitter conflicts culminating in one of the most terrible wars the world had ever known—the thirty years' war—from 1618 to 1648. Having its origin largely because of religious differences, before its close almost every possible issue, political and economic as well as religious, entered in. While the war centered in Germany almost every country in Western Europe became involved at least to some extent. Something of the horrors that resulted from it may be indicated by the fact that during these thirty years the population of Germany decreased from 16,000,000 to 6,000,000 and the

poverty, sickness, and misery of the people were almost
beyond human imagination.

DEISM

It would seem no blight could be so severe as that
of the Thirty Years War. But another blight soon followed that for nearly two centuries affected more people, and many of them more disastrously even than that
of war. I refer to deism. That was distinctly an intellectual and spiritual war—a struggle of rationalism
against the supernatural. There were many shades of
opinion, but in general the position taken was that some
sort of God might or might not have had something to
do with the creation of the world, but that at any rate
he had exercised little or no supervision since. That is
to say, they did not believe in a personal God and
Father who watched over and cared for His children.

The two most notable deists of the world were Voltaire of France and Frederick the Great of Prussia.
Both men were of unusual natural ability, and both had
had excellent training. Both were vain, egotistic, selfish, and in godlessness they stretched deism to the limit.
Voltaire saw the corruption of the Church organization,
and deplored, as much as a man of his character could,
its oppression of the poor. But having no Christian experience he was not able to see beneath the corruption
the solid foundation of the Church. Having a pleasing
style he wrote voluminously against the Church and
the Bible, and was conceited enough to think that his
onslaughts would bring about their annihilation. He

and Frederick greatly admired each other because of the similarity of their views. Frederick who had considerable worldly culture took pride in having at his Court for long periods distinguished men, especially authors, artists, and musicians. He naturally invited the witty and scintillatingly brilliant Voltaire, and felt greatly honored at his acceptance. Voltaire likewise felt greatly honored to be invited. The visit lasted thirty months—until they could endure each other no longer. However, they retained their friendship in a way until the death of Voltaire.

HOW GERMANY GOT THAT WAY

Germany, as we think of it, was for centuries divided into many small governmental units. One of these was Prussia, a duchy which, because of a succession of able rulers, had become quite strong. Frederick William, known as the "Great Elector," had a long and prosperous reign. His son, Elector Frederick, succeeded in being recognized as a King. Frederick Wm. I, the son of this King, in spite of many eccentricities, was a very successful ruler. He built up an army of 80,000 men including a regiment of very tall soldiers, and also added considerably to his dominions. At his death in 1740 his son came to the throne as Frederick II. Because of his ability, courage, forcefulness, and achievements he came to be called "the Great." Because the influence of his life and work are being seen and felt throughout the world today he needs special consideration here.

His unscrupulous action in rapaciously taking Silesia from Austria was one of the causes of the terrible and

bloody seven years war. This came at a critical period
in the struggle between England and France for colonial possession in America and India. France was
much more deeply involved in the seven year's war
than was England, and that fact gave England a great
advantage in her colonial conflict. But for this, and the
further fact mentioned elsewhere with regard to the
Huguenots France might now be one of the dominant
nations of the world, and Americans a French-speaking
people. Frederick, like his ancestors, was very militant. Though greatly gifted he was not so brilliant as
Voltaire, but he had something Voltaire did not have—
power. But he wanted more power and more posses-
sions, and all his plans were centered around that
purpose. He was opposed to Christianity (though not
a persecutor) for one reason, because it would interfere with his ambitions. He now proceeds to instill
these militant and anti-christian ideas into the minds
of the young people of Russia. Even worse, he selected
free-thinkers, deists and atheists to instruct the youth
of the land. Especially did he select such for college
professors. He had a long reign of 46 years, and in that
time he had very thoroughly indoctrinated his people in
the glory of war and the principles of deism.

In the Old Testament story of Jeroboam, King of
Israel, the reference was made over and over again to
the fact that "he made Israel to sin." The ultimate result was that his nation was carried almost in its entirety into a distressing captivity. It is probably true
that in no other case in history could the same statement be made so truthfully as of Frederick the Great.
He literally led his people into paganism.

Of the German states Austria had long been the greatest and most powerful. But she had not been able to unite all of Germany under her leadership. Now under Frederick and other forceful rulers Prussia became stronger and more forceful than Austria. In 1871 King William under the leadership of his dynamic but unscrupulous minister, Bismarck, did succeed in uniting all of Germany except Austria into a greater Germany, and became the first emperor of Germany as William I. The impetus given to deism by Frederick was continued under his successors, though forms of religion were maintained, and Prussia had become to a marked degree a militant and deistic state. Not only so but its influence spread to the surrounding states until the entire German nation had become very largely Prussianized. It was in this intellectual and spiritual atmosphere that what came to be known as "higher criticism" was born. The Bible was worked over and the supernatural so worked out that the German "supermen" could accept it.

Germany was now ready to accept the philosophy of Nietzche, "denouncing all religion and treating all moral laws as a remnant of Christian superstition, cherishing the virtues of the weak." His ideal, "the overman, is to be developed by giving unbridled freedom to the struggle for existence, will seek only his own power and pleasure, and know nothing of pity."

Conditions in England were probably about as bad at one time as they were in Prussia, and the writers favoring deism were more numerous and more gifted than in Prussia. A thoughtful and scholarly author of England thus characterized this period: "The clergy no longer regarded themselves as the ambassadors of Christ, commissioned in His name to offer salvation to the world; but as orators whose office it was eloquently to recommend to their flocks Christian, or, for the most part merely moral truths, as the surest means of happiness, both in this world and the next. Patterson, the intelligent and clearsighted historian of the period, describes it as one of decay of religion, licentiousness of morals, public corruption and profaneness of language; and made the remark that those ages in which morality alone has been most spoken of, have been those in which it has been least practiced."

It has been said that society is rotten at both ends. What little sound there is, is in the middle. That was particularly true of England in the middle of the 18th century.

The upper classes, the intelligentsia, the universities had all been so seriously affected by deism that religion was to most of them but a joke. Many of the Church leaders were corrupt and drunken, and shamefully neglected their work, being interested only in the "living" as the salary was called, the living being provided directly or indirectly by the State.

At the bottom the situation was pitiful. In town and country the lower classes were generally ignorant and debased. Worst of all were the coal miners. There were no churches accessible that they could attend even if they would do so, and they grew up, as was said, as ignorant of the gospel as the pagans of Africa.

But among the middle classes there could be found some spiritual vitality. The effects of Puritanism, and especially the wholesome influence of the King James version, were still apparent, though dimmed by the prevalent corruption.

But now a very marked divergence between conditions in England and Prussia began to appear. Conditions in England rapidly became better, and in Prussia gradually and surely worse. There were four reasons for this:

1. Deism in Prussia was enthroned in power, and that power was autocratically used to advance it.

2. There was a definite purpose in Prussia that was not present in England. Frederick and his successors were ambitious for power, and watched every chance to enlarge their dominions regardless of justice and right. A Christian spirit and attitude would interfere with this purpose.

3. They zealously indoctrinated the youth of the land in these doctrines.

4. On the other hand there was a great religious revival that spread through all the English-speaking nations, inaugurated by John Wesley and a group of like-minded men.

JOHN WESLEY

John Wesley was born in 1703, the son of a clergyman of the Church of England. His father had decided ability, but his mother was greater, being indeed one of the great women of all time. He was highly educated at Oxford University, and became a clergyman of the Church of England also. He and a small group of other young men in Oxford formed a society where they met, studied the Bible, and prayed with such regularity and persistence that their fellow students called them in de-

rision "Methodists," that is, followers of a method.
Then and after taking work in the Church he yearned
for a deeper spiritual life. But for some years his de-
sires were not realized. Though he was faithful and
conscientious his ministry could in no sense be called
successful. He came to Savannah, Georgia, to preach
to the Indians, but his work there was a failure also.

On the voyage over there was a severe storm, and he
was greatly frightened as were most of the others. But
there was a group on board that had in them a calmness
and freedom from fear that was distinctly noticeable.
It was a group of Moravians, the spiritual descendants
of John Huss, who before the time of Luther had suffered martyrdom for his faith. Never a large denomination they have been spiritual and missionary leaders
for several centuries. Wesley now sought to find the
source of their spirituality. Sometime, later, after his
return to London while listening to one of their number reading he tells us that at a quarter to nine in the
evening his "heart was strangely warmed." This was
in one of the Moravian meetings in Aldersgate Street,
and as representing a higher stage in his Christian life
is very important. But if that had remained the high
water mark of his spiritual life we would scarcely be
interested in writing or reading about him now.

JOHN WESLEY RECEIVES BAPTISM OF THE HOLY GHOST

But fortunately there is more to tell. The next eight
months constituted an epochal period. He spent some
weeks among the Moravians in Europe. On his return
he attended prayer meetings that a group of like-minded men and women were holding. The warmth of their

hearts drew them together. Sometimes whole nights were spent in prayer.

"*On the first night of* 1739," says Wesley himself, "*Mr. Hall, Kinchin, Whitefield, Hutchins and my brother Charles, were present at one love feast, with about sixty of our brethren. About three in the morning, as we were continuing instant in prayer, the power of God came mightily amongst us, insomuch that many cried out for exceeding joy, and many fell to the ground. As soon as we were recovered a little from the awe and amazement at the presence of His Majesty, we broke out with one voice, 'We praise Thee, O God, we acknowledge Thee to be the Lord.'*"

I think it may be safely said that never since the first pentecost has any other meeting been of such far-reaching importance. Here indeed were all the marks of the first pentecost except tongues of fire and the special gifts of speech, and in this case there was evidently no need of the first, and certainly not of the latter.

Immediately, without at all realizing what would be the wide-spreading extent of it, he inaugurated a work that was to become the greatest spiritual awakening of modern times. He had no idea of founding a new Church. His purpose was to purify his own Church, the Church of England. But in the providence of God he was to bring renewed spiritual vitality to all the churches, and to become the founder of the Methodist Church, whose ministry would extend to every part of the world.

It has been said that he did not lay emphasis on doctrines as much as he did on Christian experience. He did lay great emphasis upon experience. But experience must have a foundation of doctrine, and he stood emphatically for certain doctrines. *He believed and taught that Jesus died for every man, and that it is possible for every man to be saved.* He and his preachers went out and preached that doctrine throughout the land. These sermons were strongly reinforced by that great hymn of Charles Wesley:

> Come, sinners, to the gospel feast;
> Let every soul be Jesus' guest;
> Ye need not one be left behind;
> For God hath bidden all mankind.

That message in sermon and song got hold of the masses of England, drove away dark despair, and brought to them hope and good cheer.

But he went further. He believed and taught in a world still in the fogs of deism that one may have a deep and abiding religious experience; that he may receive the forgiveness of his sins, and *know it*. There was one other outstanding doctrine, but the situation today is such that it may not inappropriately be called the lost doctrine of Methodism. This will be considered later. He was fortunate in his co-workers: His brother, Charles, the great hymn writer; George Whitefield, one of the greatest orators the world has ever known, and a powerful gospel preacher; John Fletcher, the learned theologian, and others. Then, too, his mother lived several years, and her saintly wisdom helped to guide his course safely along some difficult ways.

The Wesleys and Whitefield began preaching in the

Church in which they had been brought up and in which they had been ordained clergymen, the Church of England. But they exhibited so much "enthusiasm" (fanaticism is the term we would now use for the same thought) that the doors of the Churches were soon closed to them. When Epworth Church, over which his father had presided for many years, was closed to him, John Wesley stood on his father's tomb and preached. Preaching in the open air seemed about as bad as enthusiasm, and even Wesley and his group themselves were at first shocked at the thought of it. But starting unplanned the effects were so favorable that its continuance was inevitable. The audiences increased in size until it was not unusual for Whitefield and Wesley to preach to audiences of between ten and twenty thousand people. In the summer they often preached at four o'clock in the morning, the summer days in England being long. The people were profoundly affected. Among the coal miners the tears made channels down their coal blackened faces.

Some of these men recently converted felt moved to speak and tell of the power of the gospel as it had been manifested in their own lives and those of their fellows. And they did speak. But Wesley was shocked at this for he was obsessed with the idea that for one to so speak he must be ordained by a bishop whose ordination could be traced back to the Apostles. But his mother saw the power of God so manifested by such messages that she advised John that she was convinced it was of God. And so the movement went forward, and increasing numbers of preachers were carrying their melting messages up and down the land.

All this was not done easily. There was much persecution. Wesley in his travels was often hungry and cold, and occasionally was pelted with rotten tomatoes, rotten eggs, and even stones.

But England was revolutionized—spiritually, morally, socially, economically, politically, educationally. Conditions became so changed that the corrupt and atheistic Walpole could be succeeded by the noble Pitt, as England's prime minister. It is generally agreed by historians that because of this revival England escaped a terrible revolution such as engulfed France.

Along with the profound spiritual movement there came the series of inventions, such as the steam engine, the spinning jenny, the power loom in England and the cotton gin in America, that ushered in the great industrial revolution, and made England the manufacturing center of the world. It staggers the imagination to conceive the possible baneful results of this vast increase of production and power without the humanizing effects of this spiritual power in the lives of employers and employees alike.

REVIVALS IN AMERICA

COLONIAL PERIOD

The first settlers of New England came because of religious persecution in their own country, and have generally been given credit for great piety. However, a large proportion of them were not pious enough to join the Church. But as a whole they could be considered a pious group. Their subsequent history showed them to be narrow and intolerant. Pennsylvania was settled by the Quakers, and Maryland by the Catholics, though their settlers were not limited to these groups. The other states were settled by those to whom religion was only an incidental consideration, and most of them made but slight pretension to religion. The ambition of most of them was for more bottom land and better bottom land. It is interesting to note, however, that later when evangelistic movements spread over the country some of those sections that had seemed least religious responded most readily to the earnest appeals of those who would call them back to God.

While there were no widespread revivals during the colonial period, there were able and consecrated individuals and groups in all the principal denominations who by their spiritual power and unquenchable enthusiasm laid sound spiritual foundations for the great work of subsequent years.

Reference has been made on other pages to the evil of German rationalism. But a complete story is not secured without some account of the far-reaching results of German pietism. The Moravians directly through their settlements, and indirectly through others have exerted a vast influence for good. America is greatly indebted to this pietistic influence for another movement inaugurated by Theodore J. Frelinghuysen in New Jersey. The Dutch Reformed Church in the United States did not want anything more than a formal religion, and when Frelinghuysen began to urge the importance of an inner experience and spiritual living he was bitterly opposed by the pulpit and pew of his Church. But he continued to preach and

write with such impassioned earnestness that largely
through his efforts the Dutch Reformed Church became a great spiritual power in America.

Among the Congregationalists and Presbyterians
the work of Jonathan Edwards is well known. He was
not a revivalist of the regular type. But his great intellectual ability, his deep spirituality and his impassioned earnestness made him a great spiritual force.
Not so well known are the activities of Wm. Tennent
and his group in Pennsylvania. He was a preacher of
power, but his influence as a teacher was much greater.
He conducted a school for some twenty years in which
he trained a very considerable group of young Presbyterian preachers including his own sons. In this school
which his unevangelistic fellow ministers called in de-
rision "log college," literary culture was not neglected,
but the preachers sent out were particularly distinguished for their evangelistic zeal. They were bitterly opposed, however, by most of the Presbyterian
preachers, and a serious division was threatened. At
this time George Whitefield came to America, and
found in his group kindred spirits and zealous fellow-
laborers. Because of his wonderful oratory and deep
spirituality he would have been a great power anywhere, but his work in America was much greater because of the lives and labors of this group. Whitefield
made seven trips to America, preaching all the way
from Georgia to Maine. In most places the results of
his preaching were not conserved so well as by this
group. Their combined efforts were instrumental in

greatly deepening the spirituality of Presbyterianism in America.

The work of this group extended in a rather remarkable way to the South. A group of these Spirit-filled men went into Virginia and North Carolina. Of these Samuel Davies was very prominent. Highly intelligent, eloquent, deeply pious and of fine judgment, to a very marked degree he helped to mould Presbyterianism in the South. Davies was very active in his support of the College of New Jersey, later Princeton University. In 1759 he became its fourth President, succeeding Jonathan Edwards. Another great figure of this period was Alexander Craighead of North Carolina. Distinguished as a preacher and educator he was also one of the notable leaders in the early struggles for American independence.

The Baptists in later years became so zealous in revivals that it is a little difficult to realize that in this early period the "Regular Baptists" were opposed to any vigorous evangelism. Two men, Shubal Stearns and Daniel Marshall, went from Connecticut to what is now West Virginia. They were opposed by the "Regular Baptists," and moved to Sandy Creek in Guilford County, North Carolina, and this became the center of the Separate Baptists of the South. Here may be found the source to a very considerable extent of the remarkable growth and spiritual vitality of the Baptist Church in the South.

In the Protestant Episcopal Church there was one man who should be mentioned in this connection, Devereux Jarrett. He received a definite religious esxperience, and as a result became an evangelistic power. He co-operated freely with the revivalistic Presbyterians and Methodists, and was largely influential in making the Episcopal Church in Virginia "low Church."

At the outbreak of the Revolution the Methodists had just gained a foothold in America, and were held in some suspicion because of their English connections. But that did not prove to be serious. The early Methodist preachers from England brought with them a satisfying religious experience and an unquenchable zeal to save the lost. Aside from this they had another advantage over those of similar spirit in the older denominations—they were not forced to do their work against the opposition of their own ecclesiastical organization. They were all engaged in the all-absorbing task of soul saving. Not hindered by this handicap it was natural for them to take the leadership in the great revivals of the next period.

A REBORN AMERICA

A little before the opening of the 19th century there began a spiritual awakening in America that was destined to become notable among the religious movements of the world. Among the outstanding reasons for it three may be especially noted.

1. A solid foundation for it was laid by the brave and consecrated individuals and groups as indicated above.

2. The great Wesleyan revival in England overflowed into America.

3. The need was so great that earnest men and women felt that they must have divine help.

America's condition was perhaps not so bad as that

of England a half century earlier, but the spiritual condition of the people was distressingly low. The Revo-
lutionary War had been demoralizing; there were few
churches and preachers for the widely scattered population. The fact that they had migrated from many
different sections, and had come to a new land, with
new and hitherto unknown neighbors and thus released
from former moral associations and restraints, also
tended to make them more careless as to religion. Then,
too, there were the evil effects of rationalism. The
deistic teachings of England had gone over to France,
and they had in many cases become atheistic. This
combination of deism and atheism, because of the
friendly relationship of France and the United States,
had affected tremendously the educated classes of
America, and percolated through the other classes all
the way to the bottom.

The hearts of the people were sad and lonely. A
message of hope and encouragement from any source
would be welcome. Such a message was about to be
given, but from sources that most learned men in the
quiet of the study would never have thought of. It
was to come by the labors of an uneducated ministry
in the proclamation of a winsome gospel message. The
Baptists and Methodists proved to be the principal
messengers. Their purpose was similar, but their
method was different. When the consciousness of sins
forgiven brought peace to the heart there often went
with it the impulse to tell others. The Baptist so moved
would work during the week on the farm, and then on
Sunday would go as far as he could walk or on horseback to preach to such a group as could be gotten to-

gether. Then when the crops were laid by in summer
he would have a meeting of a week or two.

The Methodist who felt moved to tell the story went
at it differently. He got a license to preach, and a
horse, and would be appointed to a circuit, maybe
some hundreds of miles away. He would go from place
to place preaching every day in the week except Mon-
day when he would rest and get his clothes washed. He
would thus preach from twenty to thirty times a month,
each day at a different place. The people would offer
him their rude hospitality for himself and horse, and a
pittance with which he would buy clothes and an occasional book. But the Bible was his constant companion, and almost his only library. On the long horseback
journeys he would read and think and pray. Everywhere there was the call to repentance, and the offer
of salvation. They preached for results and usually had
them. They preached one sermon day after day for a
month, often improving it with each repetition. He
would do the same the next month with the same message in a new setting. Then, during the summer they
would hold a series of "big meetings." These preachers
were at the beginning mostly young men. Through
summer's heat and winter's cold, through rain and
snow, through long lonely trails in sparsely settled sections, often swimming swollen streams, they seldom failed to keep an appointment. They could not in
the early days marry and settle down and enjoy the
pleasures of home life. They were not burned at the
stake nor beheaded but the lives of most of them were
shortened by the privations and hardships they endured. They often died far from home, and sometimes

no stone even gives the date of their birth and death. But they left enduring monuments in the hearts of men, women and children that were transformed by their labors. Their great leader was Bishop Francis Asbury, ordained by Wesley and sent over to America from England. He was not a great scholar like Wesley, but he had qualities that peculiarly fitted him for leadership in this new country. Sixty times he crossed on horseback the Alleghenies and was surpassed probably by no one in labors, hardships and suffering.

The doctrines of Methodism and its aggressive organization peculiarly suited the needs of the young nation of the West. It was glorious news that Jesus died for every man. Then, as increasing numbers had the heart-warming experience of the dispensation of the Son, and the heart-burning experience of the dispensation of the Holy Spirit, (or sanctification as they usually called it) new spiritual fires were started wherever they went. Churches, schools, homes, court-houses, brush arbors, and soon camp meetings were the centers from which these glowing messages poured. The camp meeting was distinctively American, and its influence for good can scarcely be over-emphasized.

These meetings affected every part of America then settled, and it is probably not too much to say that because of them the spiritual level of America became the highest of any nation in the history of the world.

In 1821, Charles G. Finney, a young lawyer of New York State, was converted. Almost immediately after, he received the baptism of the Holy Spirit. His own experience was so wonderful, and affected such a change in him that a great revival broke out in his little

town. This movement spread out and continued until
New York State, Ohio, and several neighboring states
were so moved that it was estimated that 250,000 people
were converted under his ministry.

An unusual and largely leaderless meeting occurred
in 1858, but was mostly confined to a few important
eastern cities. Beginning in 1872 the Moody and San-
key meetings stirred the whole country. In the South
and West the Sam Jones and George Stuart meetings
exerted a vast influence for good. Hundreds of other
evangelists have labored with great effectiveness.

The beneficent results of these great meetings were
not confined to the city or community in which the
meetings were conducted, but preachers and other religious workers attended from time to time from many
other sections, and securing a renewal of spiritual fervor, returned home to extend the God-given blessings
to many other groups. One of the great benefits of
these city-wide meetings was that they got nearly
everybody singing spiritual songs. These could be
heard not only in the great auditorium, but in the home,
and store, and factory, and on the street cars, trains and
sometimes on the streets. Newspapers, too, greatly extended the service by giving much space to its messages
and work.

In the great work of soul-saving the evangelist cannot do the most effective work without the co-operation
of the pastors, and it is a matter of common knowledge
that the greatest soul winners among the pastors are
most zealous in securing the co-operation of evangelists, knowing that evangelists can do with their help
what they cannot do alone.

It is true that some of the evangelists have been justly subject to criticism, especially that the meetings were too greatly commercialized. But it is really remarkable that so many, when all the facts are known, have been above serious criticism of any sort. It is a laborious life, and few will be willing to undertake it unless impelled to do so by a divine compulsion.

These meetings from the earliest period and all through the years have been the inspiration of every sort of religious and humanitarian effort.

RACE, COLOR, AND RELIGION

At no time in the past have problems of race and color been discussed so vigorously and earnestly as is being done today. Too often the discussion leaves out religion, and that cannot be left out in any adequate discussion. In the black belt in Africa there is comparative quiet. In China and Japan there has been a terrible war. Fortunately for us the two nations were arrayed against each other, and not both against us.

In India the whole country is like a volcano threatening eruption. The people are so numerous—nearly three times as many as in the United States—the country so great and varied, and the problems so intricate and complicated that an entire volume could tell but a small part of the story. This much may be said, that all the serious problems of India have their origin in religion. Approximately two-thirds of the people are Hindus, and one-third Mohammedans. These two groups are so hostile to each other that it seems impossible for them to co-operate in any great task, especially in government. One of the most serious results of both

religions is the degradation of women. Almost equally
as serious is the caste system among the Hindus. There
are four principal castes and many more subdivisions.
The lowest of these, the "untouchables" constitute
about a fourth of the Hindu population, and their lot in
life is miserable beyond our power to imagine. One of
the higher castes receives ceremonial pollution by the
touch or even the shadow of one of the untouchables.

As bad as conditions are today they were much
worse before the country became subject to England.
Bishop Thoburn, who spent most of a long and useful
life there said some years ago: "War was chronic. Every
year in the month of October there were three great
armies that marched out of the old Mahratta Capital in
Western India; one army going north, one south, and
the third east. They went to roam and to kill; they destroyed cities and overran provinces. Annually for
many years India had that scourge. They used to be in
a state of war all the time. There is a difference today;
for everywhere the Briltish flag is recognized throughout that vast empire, and among more than three
hundred millions of people there are no wars." England has done much for India. But the Indians are a
people of great possibililties and naturally desire independence. It is charged, too, that they have been exploited by England, and there is no doubt but that
there are grounds for that charge. However, it seems
reasonably certain that India has developed more sat-
isfactorily under British rule than would have been
possible in any other way. There has been and is hope
for the ultimate betterment of India only through the
Christian religion. Though the number of Christians

In India is not large, Christian influences have permeated the country to a very encouraging extent, and it may be sufficient to break down some hitherto impregnable walls.

THE NEGRO IN AMERICA

Our own racial situation is not nearly so large as that of India, but it is for us more important. While there was much cruelty and other evils connected with the enslavement of the Negroes it is nevertheless not difficult to believe that in a most wonderful way some of God's great purposes have been thereby carried out. The Negroes in Africa were pagans, and most of them very superstitious and degraded. Now in America there are 13,000,000 Negroes civilized and Christianized. Even though the civilization and Christianity are not of the highest type, nevertheless the change in them is nothing less than marvelous. We may safely say that the Negroes in great numbers could not have come to America and settled down except in the way they did come—in physical bondage. This is not so bad as it sounds without an understanding of the background, for a large proportion of them were slaves in Africa and under harder conditions than most of them had to endure in America.

Once in this country they had their opportunity. Have they made good use of it? That they have made the best possible use of this opportunity no one could claim. Nevertheless it cannot be denied that as a people they have made tremendous strides. If this had been accomplished by missionaries sent to Africa the religious world would have been astonished and delighted beyond measure. It was accomplished by Christian agencies and influences in America, though most people have not so considered it. The more one delves in to the history of these years the clearer this becomes. During those days when the hearts of the white people were being moved by the power of the gospel as preached in the homes, under brush arbors or in churches large and small the Negroes were to be found on the outskirts, at the back of the Church or in the galleries, and the stirring gospel message that was used of the Holy Spirit to move the hearts of the white man was also used by the same Spirit to move the hearts of the black man as well. In sermon, prayer and song there was the frequent use of "Our Father." This meant that in spite of color and condition they and their white masters were brothers, and though there might be bondage of the body there were no bonds that could bind the soul. They also heard that Jesus died for every man, and that salvation was possible for them without money and without price. Many of them looked to Jesus in faith and found by experience that these messages were true, and they went back to their daily tasks with a light heart.

On the large plantations the blacks greatly outnumbered the whites, and to these missionaries, especially Baptist and Methodist, were sent. Some of these were very able men, such, for example, as young W. C. Capers who later became an honored Bishop of the Methodist Church. Then, too, the divine afflatus touched not a few slaves who though without book knowledge had a story to tell, a story of salvation. In a crude and humble way that story was told to black groups, and other hearts crude and humble were touched. Here and there arose from their number a preacher of great eloquence and deep spiritual power, who delighted white as well as black audiences with their ministry.

There was Ralph Freeman of Anson County, North Carolina, a slave until in mature life his friends purchased his freedom. Old Rocky River Church was the leading Baptist Church in a large section of country. The pastor, a man of ability, was elected to the Congress of the United States. In his absence several months each year for several years Ralph served this church as a supply pastor. He was in great demand over a wide territory for funerals and special occasions. On one occasion he went on horseback several hundred miles to Tennessee to preach the funeral of a white Baptist preacher friend, all expenses paid and a generous purse besides. A white man who never heard him, but who had heard from older lips the story of his beautiful life placed a marble marker at his grave in Ansonville, North Carolina.

Another man even more remarkable was Henry Evans, a full-blooded Negro. He was a free Negro (probably born free), a shoemaker by trade. Converted at an early age in Virginia, he soon felt the call to preach. At maturity he went into upper North Carolina where he stayed for a year. He then set out for Charleston, South Carolina where he proposed to locate. Stopping at Fayetteville, North Carolina, he was stirred by the godlessness of the place, and was so encouraged by the response to his appeals that he decided to locate there. He preached on the outskirts of the town, and the Negroes flocked to hear him. The white people were naturally suspicious of Negroes gathering in large numbers.   But they soon noticed that those who attended were not made worse but very much better.   Such glowing reports were brought back by the Negroes that some whites went out.   Soon he was preaching to the whites as well as to the blacks.   The good news that he brought with such eloquence and spiritual power was the beginning in that section of the great spiritual revival that was destined during the early years of the 19th century to revolutionize the spiritual life of the nation.   Bishop Capers said he was the best preacher of his time in that section.

One of the immediate results of his work there was the founding of the white Methodist Church.   This writer's great-great-grandmother was one of the eight charter members.

His last message was a fitting close to a great life. Leaning on the altar rail he said very simply: "I have come to say my last word to you.   It is this: None but Christ.   Three times I have had my life in jeopardy for preaching the gospel to you, and if in my last hours I could trust to anything else but Christ crucified for my salvation all should be lost and my soul perish forever." It has been truly said that this message was worthy of the Apostle Paul.

It is not only in the distant past that such Christian noblemen in black lived.   But recently there went to his eternal reward George W. Carver, born in slavery, but who came to be honored throughout the world as a scientist; and honored nowhere more than in his own South not only as a scientist but as a saint.

These and similar cases do not tell the full story.

There are multitudes whom the gospel has never effectively reached—multitudes, indeed, who have never really gotten away from African paganism. One pathetic situation has developed among these. There have here and there arisen from their own ranks religious racketeers who for money and glory have shamefully exploited their followers.

The great mass of Negroes are between these two groups. The proportions of each group vary very considerably in different sections. There are many who are inclined to judge all by the noblest examples; there are many others who would judge all by those at the bottom. Both are wrong, and the Negroes themselves and the world suffer because of these pre-judgments. But all who with unbiased minds have seen the various angles of the subject are glad to testify to their marvelous development through the years.

But this development of the Negroes has not been without cost to the whites. This has been especially in three particulars:

1. Slavery greatly retarded educational opportunity for the masses of the white people. The wealthy and even well-to-do could have tutors and send their children away to boarding schools and colleges. The educational opportunities for the poor white people were exceedingly limited.

2. The white people got the idea that manual labor was slave's work. They were losing the glorious conception of the dignity of labor, an irreparable loss to any individual or people.

3. They were developing in wide sections into a caste system among the white people that threatened

to become rigid. The slave-owning, cultured and the non-slave owning, uncultured were drifting apart in a way perilous for a great civilization.

The time came when physical bondage for the blacks had served its purpose, and the slaves needed their freedom. This might have been secured without war. But the whites needed to be freed from the dangers indicated above. We do not know what might have been, but we do know that the rich man and the poor man fought together on the battlefield and came out with a devotion each to the other that ever after drew them together. The war laid a secure foundation for white solidarity. But more was needed. Given the ballot before they were ready for it the Negroes became the political victims of designing, corrupt white men from the North and the South, and the South was in serious danger of being inundated with floods of ignorance and corruption. Again the white man of culture had to call upon the unprivileged white to stand with him in this new crisis. The uncultured white man nobly responded to the call, and they have stood together through the years. We may be profoundly thankful to God that a deadening caste system among the whites has been averted. The poverty and struggle of the war and reconstruction during the following years made necessary for nearly everybody a good deal of manual labor and gradually if slowly we have been learning the dignity and glory of it. The years since have been years of peace, quietness, and gradual development for both races. Many of the old affections between the races have persisted.

That is something that only those who have experienced it can understand. Southern white people have helped the Negroes more in the building and support of churches, and Northern white people more with boarding schools and colleges. The better elements among both races have generally worked and planned together harmoniously. Never elsewhere in the history of the world have two races, so numerous, so different in background and culture, and living and working together so closely, gotten along so pleasantly.

But during and since World War II there have come decided changes in condition and view point. The Negroes have received much more money than they have ever had before, much of it directly or indirectly from the Government. Certain situations became so serious that their very sincere and greatly gifted friend, Mr. Roger W. Babson, a New Englander who spends his winters in Florida, recently wrote them an open letter that was widely publicized. In this letter he chided them for not saving their money and especially for their refusal to work even though for three or four times the usual wage. One especial weakness not mentioned by Mr. Babson has been particularly exasperating to employers. Many have shown a lack of dependability in regularity of work. Knowing they can get another job any time they have not hesitated to stay away from work a day or two or altogether without notice whenever it suited them. This, of course, is not true of all. Many have measured up to the highest standards during these critical years. But many have so signally failed that they have because of it lost much of the sympathy that most people have had for them. Foolish, even though sincere, ideologists and corrupt and designing politicians have been responsible for much of this. To make one dissatisfied with the only work he or she can do without providing any other is criminal.

What does the future hold in store for the Negro? It is hazardous to make predictions about any social situation, because so many elements of uncertainty enter in. But for various reasons, more especially economic, very diligent study and investigation have been made by trained research workers, and in view of the information they gained the following seems very probable: It now seems that of necessity the South is destined to undergo changes that will affect every phase of life. While other great agricultural sections of the country have long ago developed mechanized farming the South has retained handwork methods, especially in cotton. Now competition from foreign countries with cheap labor, and the rapid development of synthetics make it imperative that cotton must be produced more cheaply. At the same time inventions and discoveries of recent years have made it possible to cultivate and gather cotton by machinery with only a fraction of the labor necessary by hand labor. The Negro who has skill enough to plow with a tractor instead of a mule will have a job at increased pay running tractors and other machinery. The one who has dependability sufficient for the care of live stock will find profitable work in this field. Others with initiatve will be happy in the production and processing of fruits and vegetables. All these occupations will require a higher order of intelligence and dependability than growing cotton by the old methods. The positions will be ready for those capable of filling them. For this labor, too, there will be larger compensation, and that in turn will make possible higher standards of living and greatly increased self-respect without foolish arrogance. A considerable portion of the unskilled and less dependable workers may be used in various capacities.

It is not at all likely that racial solidarity will be disturbed. All the white people and most of the Negroes believe it would be unwise to do so. But there will be much greater opportunities, not only as indicated above, but for business and professional groups as well. Especially will there be a great opportunity for well-trained preachers, teachers, doctors, dentists and nurses. Comparatively recent developments are opening up for them another field of very great opportunity, viz., a service that may come under the general classification of welfare work. This group will include men and women who will go to the homes and farms and help the workers with their domestic and vocational problems. Enough has already been done in these activities to indicate the great possibilities for the future.

It may be said that these were the ideals that sustained Booker T. Washington, George W. Carver and others of like spirit. Though ideologists have now gotten the heads of many Negroes filled with foolish and perfectly impracticable and impossible notions, may it not seem but a reasonable optimism to expect a much brighter day ahead along lines that are desirable and possible. Better living conditions and public conveniences which thoughtful white people are now demanding for them will be gradually supplied.

But it is believed that with the coming of these

changes there will be large numbers of unskilled workers thrown out of employment, some estimating that
these may number during the next few years as many
as two millions. What will become of them?

When Negroes were first brought to America they
could not stay in the North because that section could
not profitably use such unskilled labor. So they went
South where it could be so used. Since the War between the States quite a large number of Negroes have
gone from the South to the North. These for the most
part have been from the better and more intelligent
element. It seems now, however, that this situation
will be reversed. The better element will remain in the
South, and the poor, unskilled element will by necessity go to the big cities of the North and West where
they will fill menial jobs in industrial plants, and do
heavy public work formerly done by foreign immi-
grants. If this occurs as now seems likely it will constitute one of the greatest voluntary and peacetime mi-
grations of history, and many of the most serious problems of race will thus automatically be shifted from the
South to the North.

In all our discussions of this subject we need to remember that it is the Christian religion that has enabled these two races to live together peacefully all
these years; and we must not fail to realize that it alone
will enable us to live peacefully together in the years
to come.

FOREIGN MISSIONS

The evangelistic meetings in England and America
inspired the Christians with a fresh determination to

become obedient to our Lord's last command, to carry the gospel to all the world. Missionary societies were formed by all the leading denominations to carry the gospel to India, to China, to Japan, to Africa, to the islands of the sea. Bible Societies were formed to translate the Bible into the different languages of the world. Their success has been phenomenal. The Bible as a whole has been translated into all the leading languages, and in whole or in part into more than a thousand languages and dialects.

When this began it took rare courage and spiritual discernment even to contemplate the enormous task of world evangelism. In addition to the barriers of language as just indicated which have been gradually broken down through the years, there were the barriers of race, of customs, of entrenched evil, of distance, of closed doors on the foreign front, and on the home front indifference and financial weakness. When William Cary, the Baptist missionary, went to India in 1807 he was refused by the East India Company admission as a missionary. He unhesitatingly entered in as a common laborer. He lived to be recognized as one of the greatest linguists, and noblest men not only of India, but of the world. It warms one's heart as he contemplates how some of the great evils have fled before the light and warmth of the gospel; slavery; binding feet; suttee, that is, women burned with their dead husbands; cannibalism; and many others. It would require a volume simply to enumerate the marvelous experiences of the missionaries in every part of the world.

Towards the latter part of the 19th century the situation seemed so bright that a great student movement was inaugurated with the slogan: "The world for Christ in this generation." Never before had there seemingly been such a combination of circumstances to encourage.

But just when it seemed that not only would mission work be successfully carried to every land, but would be of a higher type than had generally prevailed there arose difficulties of a very serious nature. A new conflict of rationalism against the supernatural developed.

MODERNISM

As Modernism had its origin mostly in Germany, it is important to notice just what had been happening there during this period. First of all there was no revival. There has been no general religious awakening in Germany nor in any continental country since the time of Luther, Calvin and Zwingli. Not only that but in Germany the tendency has been strongly in the opposite direction. It has been said that often a business, institution, or country is the lengthened shadow of a man. To a very marked degree Prussia and ultimately Germany was the lengthened shadow of Frederick the Great. His mad passion for power to be secured by military force, and his strenuous opposition to any belief in the supernatural, together became the predominant characteristics of Germany. The German people had long been used to struggle and hardship. That fact together with the fact that they are a very virile people enabled them during a period of peace to surge forward rapidly in material development and in secular education.

But during all this time they never lost sight of these aims: a great army, material prosperity, secular education and religious views that would not interfere with ambitious designs for increased power and expansion. As they enlarged their dominions, multiplied their resources, and increased their knowledge, especially the physical sciences, their ambitions also moved forward at an accelerating pace. They now became obsessed with the idea of becoming the dominating power of Europe, and ultimately of the world.

But the thing that they seemed to take most pride in was their ingenius reconstruction of the Bible. By diligent and learned research they found by their own confession that the Bible was not given by divine inspiration. Nor did it have divine authority, but was largely a series of purely human documents written several hundred years after they were supposed to have been written by a group of ambitious and scheming priests to bolster their own power and prestige, and that it was palmed off on a gullible people, and accepted by them and succeeding generations. This palpable fraud was never even suspected by any of the saints and scholars of the past. But now the German supermen uncovered it and revealed it to a waiting world. All this seems like a fairy tale. But we know that it has actually happened. We know, too, that it fits into German nature, experience and history.

Nor is it surprising with their lordly notions of superiority that they should inaugurate a system of propaganda—German ability, German knowledge, German efficiency, and especially their superior knowledge of the Bible. The surprising thing is that England, Scotland and America with their marvelous background of vital religious experience should accept this propaganda at its face value, but the simple fact is that multitudes of them did, and hundreds of bright young ministerial students from these countries treked to Germany to secure the "scientific viewpoint" of the Bible. The term deism by this time had come to have an unsavory reputation, so a new name was found, "modernism." The substance was the same, but the form was different. Previous attacks had been against some phases of Christianity. This was against its central reservoir of power, a stab at the very heart of the Bible, and what the Bible stands for.

An ancient question in time of perplexity was, "Watchman, what of the night?" That question has often been asked as to our night of perplexity. For a long time the answer was a confused one. The situation is clarifying—The German military ambitions have met a terrible defeat. They lost the first World War but did not admit defeat. What they needed, according to their thought, was quicker action and greater ruthlessness and barbarity. That has now failed. Millions of their men are dead on the field of battle. Their cities are in ruins. National humiliation and disgrace, it would seem, must make them amenable to reason.

What of their claim of superior Biblical knowledge? Ideas are more powerful than bullets and bombs, but they are slower acting. The Germans will fail on this intellectual and spiritual battlefield, just as surely as they have failed on the physical battlefields of Europe and Africa. But while it is now apparent that this new phase of rationalism will lose out as in the case of Arianism and deism, in the meantime the effect upon the Christian countries has been like a freezing wintry blast upon tender vegetation. We may express the hope that another widespread pentecostal experience may sweep away all in these movements that are untrue and hurtful and leave us more deeply entrenched in our confidence in the personal protection and guidance of our Lord. It may be that the dread ordeal through which we have been passing may have an important influence in this great work.

Thus we can see at a glance the successes and failures of the Church through the centuries. There were periods when considerable numbers of people had received the baptism of the Holy Spirit, and whenever and wherever that was the case we would see a rapid expansion of religious activity and development. Under such conditions much larger numbers would also come into the dispensation of the Son, that is, they would have a sense of pardoned sins, though they would not have the spiritual power of those in the dispensation of the Holy Spirit. Even at such times perhaps a much larger number would still be in the dispensation of the Father, and the type of their religious life would be very similar to that of Old Testament times.

But there were other periods—often long extended periods—when the number in the two higher groups was very small. At such times most of those whose faces were turned Godward at all would be in the dispensation of the Father, and the spiritual tone of the world would be low.

Is it true that a large proportion of the people of the

world are in the dispensation of the Father, especially in times when interest in religion is low?   Is it true among heathen nations that know little of God, and show it by low living?   Or is it true that as they seem hopelessly without God in this world, that they will be shut off from Him forever.

Let us keep these questions before us in the next section.

A TRIUMPHANT TRIO: KNOWLEDGE, CONSE-
CRATION, FAITH

A Triumphant Trio:
Knowledge, Consecration, Faith

The general principles of spiritual development
have been discussed. If we were dealing with inani-
mate substances this would be sufficient. But we are
dealing with human beings. That means diversity. For
ages people spoke of the seven wonders of the world
but in these modern times there are so many wonders
that it would be difficult to keep count of them. Yet
all the time and even to this day there were two wonders not generally spoken of as such, but were vastly
greater than those generally so considered. One of
these is that every leaf of every forest is so far as
known different from every other leaf. The other is
that every human being is different from every other,
and in addition each one changes from moment to moment, and just now is somewhat different from every
previous moment, and is likewise different from what
he will be in any future moment. No study can be
completed without the consideration of individual differences and idiosyncrasies, whether from heredity, en-
vironment, or the grace of God.

We may assume that everybody begins his career
in the dispensation of the Father. I believe it will be
safe to say without argument that God gives every

128

child that good a start. If he should die in infancy we cannot imagine that he would be eternally separated from God. God has made us in His own image and after His own likeness, so that we may be worthy of companionship with Him forever. But if we are like Him we must have the power of choice. When a child comes to years of accountability he naturally makes a decision for or against God. So he may look to God in trust, or turn his back upon Him in rebellion. If he rebels against God, he loses his place in the dispensation of the Father and enrolls himself as among those who are in rebellion against God. If he trusts Him he may remain in the dispensation of the Father, or he may ascend higher on the spiritual stairway that leads to God, either into the dispensation of the Son, or still higher into the dispensation of the Holy Spirit.

As indicated in previous pages the three factors that determine what stage he will reach are: Knowledge, Consecration, and Faith. Let us consider these more fully.

KNOWLEDGE

Knowledge undoubtedly has a large place in the development of spiritual attainments. By knowledge here is not meant a varied assortment of facts and their relationship, but an understanding of God and our relationship to Him. Does everyone have some knowledge of God? It is assumed by some that vast numbers of the population of the world do not have any knowledge of God because they have not had, whether through their own fault or that of others, a revelation such as we have enjoyed. But they have no right to such an assumption. Jesus said, "And I, if I be lifted up from the earth will draw all men unto me"—all men, not just those who have heard about Him. Paul said, "They that have not the law are a law unto themselves." How many ways Jesus has of drawing men to Him we do not know, but we may be certain that He has neglected no available way. Then, too, most of us know ourselves so slightly that we are not able adequately to determine just the nature of the law within us that will leave us without excuse if not obeyed. But with the authority of Jesus, together with that of His great apostle and interpreter, St. Paul, we may say that every man has or will have knowledge enough for salvation.

It is needless to say that there is a vast difference in the degree of knowledge possessed by different individuals. It may be compared to our earthly lights. The light of the sun may be compared to the spiritual light of those of us who have had the full privilege of God's revealed will as given in His Word. The light of the moon to those where the Bible is really known only partially to individuals, or to small groups. The light of the stars is like the light among pagan peoples. However, it is very important for us to remember that there are many in our Christian countries who have but little if any more knowledge of God than those living in heathen darkness. This is a fact not generally recognized. The jocular comment that some man has been exposed to a college education has a pathetic application to many people in the matter of religion. A great many people have been exposed to religion who have but very hazy ideas about it. On the other hand, both in this land and in the darkest lands of heathenism there are certain standards of right and wrong that they have somehow secured. The standards may be very low compared with those of Christ, and may be very imperfectly kept, but it is of importance that they do have standards, and make some effort to live up to them, or feel a sense of condemnation when they do not. This does not mean that knowledge is not important, for it is absolutely necessary for the greatest happiness and usefulness. But the lack of full knowledge may not necessarily consign us to perdition. Other factors may enter into it.

JERRY MCCAULEY

This may be illustrated by the life of Jerry McCauley. As a boy he grew up in the slums of New York City. A drunken grandmother, with whom he lived, was about as low as anyone could get. He had to steal to live, and he became known as an unusually expert river thief. He says he was guilty of every sin in the decalogue, except murder, and was guilty of that many times in his heart. He was much of the time in prison. One day at a religious service in the prison a man out of the ordinary called Awful Gardner, whom Jerry knew, went to speak to them. He said, "Men, I am not worthy to stand up where the preachers stand, I'll get down here with you." He then spoke out of his heart to them, told them that he was a changed man, that he had found by experience the truth of the statement in the Bible that said the blood of Jesus Christ His Son cleanseth from all sin. Jerry was profoundly moved. He went back to his cell and took the Bible hitherto neglected to hunt the quotation the speaker used. He started in at Genesis. He didn't find it, but he found much else, and in his agony of heart he looked to Jesus and received from Him a glorious cleansing. He was so happy he could not keep quiet. Everybody in the prison learned about his experience and the effect of it was profound. He had a terrible struggle especially after he got out of prison, but he finally had victory. He established a mission in one of the worst parts of the city and for several years did a great work for God. He died at forty-five from the effects of his early sinful life. A prominent preacher was asked to conduct his funeral. As he went down he thought to himself, "Poor Jerry! There did not many people know him as I did. I am afraid there will not be many out today to his funeral." As he came near the Church where the funeral was to be held he saw the street full of people, and was disturbed, fearing a terrible accident had occurred. But he found that the Church had overflowed, and the people were massed on every side for a block or two, and men had to lift him over the shoulders of the people for him to get into the church and to the pulpit.

On the outskirts of the crowd a poor man carried a faded rose to a policeman and asked him to put it on Jerry's casket, not at all knowing or thinking that the casket was covered with many of the loveliest flowers the city could furnish. With the flower he told this story: "I had a girl about sixteen years old, and she got sick, and she knew she was going to die, and she was afraid to die. I was just a rough, sinful man, and she had never had no chance. She wanted somebody to pray for her. I did not know anybody who could do it, but someone told me about a preacher. I went to see him. He said he was sorry but he had an engagement and couldn't go. Then somebody told me of a Sunday School Superintendent. I went to see him, but he said he was so busy that he could not leave his business that day. Finally someone told me about Jerry, and I went to see him. He said, 'Yes, I will go. I don't think God will be hard on a girl like her.' He came with me and talked and prayed with her, and she became satisfied to die. I want to get you to put this rose on his casket for me." This girl on her dying bed probably accepted the first real chance she ever had to take Jesus for her Savior. Jerry, a hardened sinner, doubtless accepted the first chance he really ever had of knowing God in His pardoning power. What wonderful results came from a little knowledge. Many others have never had that kind of knowledge. But if there is a yearning in the heart for a knowledge of God even though they may not know at all what it is or what to call it, or how to satisfy it, God will in His mercy find a way to give them the knowledge, even if He has to do for them as He did for Saul of Tarsus, open the very windows of heaven to do it.

AFRICANER

Another illustration: Africaner was a wild, barbarous African native chief who took great pride in the number of human scalps he had. When the missionaries first went into his country they did so at the risk of their lives. But he was finally reached, and with the first real knowledge of God he yielded himself to Him with a beautiful humility, and became an earnest Christian. Untold millions in heathen lands do not have the revelation of God's will that means so much to many of us, but Jesus is drawing them in some way to Himself. If they yield with the slight knowledge they have to the urge for a better life our God will not turn them away for lack of full knowledge.

But it is not the down-and-outs only who do not know God. There are many among the most prominent people who have had God so misrepresented to them, perhaps by speech, certainly by actions, that they have not known where to turn to find relief for an aching heart. Somewhere and sometime and somehow if knowledge only is their need God will find a way to give them the light that they must have to secure the peace that only He can give.

FAITH

Another factor necessary for a Christian life is faith. It is interesting to note that beautiful examples of faith may be manifested in any and every stage of the religious life. Probably there is nothing more comforting to struggling, sinning humans than that God loves to hear their cry and answer their plea, it doesn't matter from what stage of spiritual experience the cry may come. Perhaps the two most touching instances of faith in the life of Jesus on earth occurred in the case of two men who according to the standards of some people would not be expected to have any religion at all, and who evidently did not claim much, if any. One, a centurion (or captain) in the Roman army had a servant who was very dear to him, and now he was sick unto death. He had done everything he could for him without result. But he had heard of Jesus; and maybe he had stood on the outskirts of the crowd and heard Him talk. He probably had seen those who had been cured by Him. He believed Jesus could heal his servant. But he felt that Jesus was too good for a rough soldier to approach, so he went to some of the friends of Jesus to intercede for him. Of course Jesus would not turn a deaf ear to a plea like that, and started at once to the house of the Captain. But the Captain stopped Him. "I am not worthy for you to come into my house. Besides, it is not necessary. Just say the word." The word was said; the servant arose from his bed a well man; the Captain's heart was filled with gratitude and humble devotion; and the heart of our Lord was comforted by this beautiful faith as it could not have been in any other way.

The other case was that of a nobleman in Capernaum, probably an official of the corrupt court of Herod. His son was about to die. The doctors and nurses had done all they could. The situation seemed hopeless. If Jesus were only there, but He was away and His family and friends did not know when He would be back. Then somebody brought the message that Jesus was at Cana, some twenty-five miles away. The nobleman did not send but went to Jesus at once, hurrying over the hills as fast as he could. He told Jesus the situation. What others could not do at all was easy for Jesus. "Thy son liveth" were the precious words that came from the lips of the Master. Did the nobleman rush home that night as he might have done? Not at all. He spent the night—probably the first good

night's rest he had had in quite awhile. The next day
he went leisurely back home, no doubt tears of gratitude streaming from his eyes at times. As he came
near his house his servants rushed forth to tell him the
good news, "Your son's well." "Yes, I know. When
did the fever leave him?" "At seven o'clock." It was
the hour when Jesus spoke. Under the circumstances
would we have stayed away, or would we have been
burdened with anxiety until we could see the romping
son with our own eyes?

GEORGE MULLER

Though profound knowledge of God, and deep consecration are not necessary to faith nevertheless they
greatly help. I will give two modern cases. George
Muller was wild in his youth, but later gave himself to
God. He was moved to put God to a test to prove to a
doubting world that there is a living, prayer-hearing
God. There was a great need. Many orphan children
were homeless. So he started an orphanage, in Bristol,
England. There was one unalterable stipulation in his
plans. He would never ask for money except from God,
and he would never tell man his needs. The money
came for building after building during the years, and
food and maintenance and instruction for the children.
And they never went hungry. One morning they did
not have enough for breakfast. He told God about it.
Just then a man brought in a large lot of milk. His
wagon had broken down in front of the orphanage, and
he said he'd just give the milk to the orphans. Muller
lived to be very old and God never once failed him. He
said that *all* things work together for good to them that

love God—not 500 times out of 1000, nor 900, but 999 times—and one more.

J. HUDSON TAYLOR

Another well-known case was Hudson Taylor of England. His parents were consecrated to God. When he was born they gave him to God for foreign work. But as he grew up he was not spiritual, and it seemed that their hopes would be frustrated. When he was sixteen his mother made a rather long visit to friends at some distance from their home. One rainy afternoon her heart being burdened for her boy, she asked her friends to let her go to her room that afternoon and be alone. She went in and with fervent prayer she laid her burden before the Lord. After some time she had the assurance that her prayer was answered, and she spent the balance of the time rejoicing. That same afternoon her boy at home was lonely and restless. He went into the attic to see if he could find a book to pass away the time. He found a small book. He said to himself he would read the story and leave the moral for some one else. But as he read he came upon one sentence that gripped him, that brought light and comfort to his troubled heart. He went to his older sister and they rejoiced together. Then he said, "Sister, don't tell mother. I want to surprise her." His sister promised. After two more joyous weeks the mother returned home. As she came he rushed to her and said, "Oh, Mother, I have good news for you." She said, "Yes, I know, my son. I have been happy over it for two weeks." He drew back and said, "Oh, Mother did sister tell you? She promised me she wouldn't tell you." Then she said, "No, your sister didn't tell me, God told me." That boy was Hudson Taylor. He founded the China Inland Mission on faith. His story sounds like a continuance of the Acts of the Apostles. In my young manhood it was my privilege to see and hear him, then an old man. It was a benediction to be so near one who had lived so near to God.

CONSECRATION

The other necessary factor of the spiritual life is Consecration. That is the crucial test. A lady said to Mr. Moody, "Oh, Mr. Moody, I'd give the world to have the spiritual power you have." Mr. Moody quickly replied, "Madam, that is what I paid for it." As there are degrees of knowledge and of faith, so there are degrees of consecration. A so-called self-made man of wealth once said to me, "No man ever gave me anything. I have worked for everything I have." I replied, "No, you haven't. Many of the things you enjoy most you haven't worked or paid for. There is your Bible. It has come to you through the agony, tears, and blood of many men. You haven't paid for it. You can never pay for it." And if the world is ever brought to Christ it will be because consecrated men and women do heart-breaking tasks for which they will never get paid in dollars and cents, in worldly ease or in worldly honor. I think of the earliest days of Christian missions when it took several months to go to China. In a storm the ship rolled so a mother with a young baby was thrown out of her berth upon the floor of the ship. Between her sobs she said, "Oh, Lord, all this I do for Thee."

Thus there are three stages of the religious life, but in each there are innumerable shadings of knowledge, faith and consecration. In each also the physical, intellectual and spiritual handicaps are different. The aspirations, hopes and fears vary with each individual during every passing hour. But in it all and through it all our one worthwhile task is to climb upward to God, and to take others with us. How is it done?

ASCENDING THE SPIRITUAL STAIRWAY

Ascending the Spiritual Stairway

As little children we start in the dispensation of the Father. Our standing here is determined not by our professions nor our deeds, but by our attitude. A mother tells her child to go to the store and get some eggs. He does it and on the return he falls and breaks half the eggs. He is sorry and is anxious to go back or do anything else he can to relieve the situation even to take the money from his little bank. His service was very poor, but his attitude fine. A mother tells another child to go to the store and get ten things. He gets nine and is well-pleased with himself. His mother says, "Where is the other article?" He said, "It wasn't convenient for me to bring that." "Now run back and get it for I need it." "No, I do not want to go back. Once is enough." His service was 90% good, but his attitude was 100% bad. So it is in our dealings with God. It is the attitude that will be pleasing or displeasing to Him more than the doing or failure to do any particular thing.

What is the spiritual condition of those in the dispensation of the Father? They have some knowledge, some consecration, some faith, but usually they live so far from God that they do not get much satisfaction out

141

of their religion. They may or may not feel much distress because of their sins. They do not have a sense of sins forgiven and of the peace which Jesus gave to His disciples and gives to all who put their trust in Him. Whom does this group include? It does not include those in conscious and determined rebellion against God nor those with a conscious sense of sins forgiven. But it includes the group between these two. It is my belief that the great mass of the peoples of the world now and in the past have belonged to this group. In saying this I am not unmindful of the saying of Jesus: Matthew 7:13, 14. "Enter ye in at the strait gate: for wide is the gate, and broad is the way that leadeth to destruction, and many there be that go in thereat; because strait is the gate, and narrow is the way which leadeth into life, and few there be that find it."

Practically all thoughtful people agree only too regretfully that Jesus stated a simple fact that we may see any day, that the multitudes are rushing headlong in an evil way. But God is not through with them yet. I remember, too, that Jesus is drawing all men unto Himself, that the Holy Spirit is praying for us with groanings that cannot be uttered; that Jesus prayed for some who were doing very badly, "Father, forgive them for they know not what they do."

I remember that many preachers have spoken plainly and forcibly of the penalties of evil doing, then when some die whose record has not been at all good, they have in most cases found some comfort for the loved ones left behind.

It has been my lot to know many kinds of people; educated and uneducated, rich and poor, workers and shirkers, Church members and non-Church members, farmers, industrial workers, tradesmen, professional groups, men, women, and children, white and black. I have had intimate personal glimpses into the lives of many of them. They certainly have not as a rule been righteous over much. In many cases they have not endeavored to excuse themselves. But most of them though were looking hopefully if somewhat doubtfully and fearfully to the future. Most of them have been weak and stumbling but not stubbornly rebellious. But the Godhead is still making every effort possible in their behalf. Men and women on the higher steps of the stairway that leads to God are co-operating by example, urgent plea and agonizing prayer. Then there is another tremendous agency often overlooked in this connection—suffering.

We may profitably consider the parable of the barren fig tree. For three years it bore no fruit. The owner instructed the dresser of his vineyard to cut it down. But the vine dresser urged the owner to try it one more year, and let him dig about and fertilize it. Multitudes of the peoples of the earth are like the barren fig tree. Suffering is one of the ways by which the digging and fertilization is accomplished. Often it is the only way that has not been tried. Physical pain, blasted hopes, disappointed aspirations we naturally dread, but they may be just what we need to save us or our loved ones from destruction.

All this constitutes life—the efforts of the Godhead in our behalf, with what co-operation we ourselves will give, and also with the hindrances that we and others too often interpose. This, too, constitutes the subject matter, however embellished, of all great and enduring literature. An excellent illustration of this is that of Silas Marner by George Eliot.

SILAS MARNER

In the days immediately before the days of the power loom a young man named Silas Marner operated a hand loom on which he wove linens. He belonged to the lower classes in England and was limited in his ability and vision, but his habits were exemplary, and his character above reproach. He was also very faithful to the Church. Another young man, also active in the Church, and he were so intimate that they were often spoken of as David and Jonathan. He was engaged to a young woman of his own class and expected soon to be happily married. With dramatic suddenness conditions changed and he was plunged into indescribable agony. A sum of money had been stolen, and his pretended friend, the real thief, managed to frame up the case against Silas. They turned him out of the Church in disgrace, and urged his betrothed to forsake him. This she did and soon after married the pretended friend. Broken hearted, Silas left and went into, for him, a distant part of the country, and set up his loom in an isolated little cottage. He felt that God could not be just and permit such a miscarriage of justice. Because of the attitude of the Church folks with whom he had had such delightful fellowship in other days he became bitter toward everybody. In his new home he kept aloof from others except to sell the product of his loom, and to buy his few necessities. Once he made a friendly overture to a neighbor but was misunderstood and made no more. Now for a fine piece of work he received a beautiful gold coin. He looked upon it with a new delight and wanted more, and yet more, until his thoughts were absorbed with it as he counted and gloated over it each night after the work on the loom was done, until he became a confirmed miser.

Then, one night his hoard of gold was stolen, and again he was cast into utter dejection. One night a short time later coming from another part of his little cottage to the front of the fireplace where his hoarded treasure had been left under some movable bricks he saw with much inner excitement a golden glint. Could it be his gold? No, no, not that, but the golden curls of a pretty two-year-old girl who had unobserved crept in out of the snow, and had fallen asleep in front of the fire. Tracing the footsteps of the child he found lying dead in the snow nearby the mother whose lot in life, though unknown to him, had been even sadder than his own.

He had not lost quite all his faith in God because he felt that God had sent the child to him to relieve his loneliness and sorrow of heart. But now he could no longer live unto himself. The child must be fed and neighborly mothers helped him. She must have clothes and other neighbors were glad to offer assistance. They told him the little one must be christened and brought up as a Christian. That took him to the minister and the Church. During all this period the little girl stroked his face and put her little arms about his neck and planted kisses upon his cheeks. Thus the joy of life cast out the bitterness, and God again became real, and the neighbors kind and true and lovable.

It is my belief that all these agencies working together will at last bring the great majority of these struggling masses into the fold of our Lord. But I must be careful not to offer hope where there is no hope. God is long suffering, but there comes a time when he is through. There cannot be any rebellion in heaven. Today we have, we know not if we shall have another.

There were two groups that Jesus did not hesitate to excoriate. First, the scribes and Pharisees. These religious teachers were more concerned about maintaining their religious organization, and in keeping their own high position than in ministering to the spiritual needs of those who looked to them for spiritual help and guidance. Centuries later when the Christian Church was at a very low ebb, Milton called the religious leaders of England "blind mouths." They were blind to the spiritual needs of their people, but their mouths were open to receive the good things of life. It is exceedingly serious for religious leaders to become corrupt, and it is serious for followers to remain quiet and complacent, and do nothing about it.

The other group that especially received the censure of Jesus were those whose god was money. Both of these sins were of a cold-blooded, calculating type. These groups adopted their course in life deliberately, and regardless of the consequences. Such men would have to have an entirely different outlook on life before they could be worthy of companionship with God. And it is not easy for such to utter the words of penitence: "God be merciful to me a sinner."

HOW LITTLE RELIGION MAY ONE HAVE?

First of all it is very clear that it is God's purpose that all should be saved. II Peter 3:9. "And the Lord is not willing that any should perish, but that all should come to repentance." What specifically was done to bring this about? We are told that God so loved the world that He gave His only begotten Son. Was it possible for Him to do more? Jesus for His part suffered humiliation and pain unto death, even the death on the cross. What more could He do? Then, too, we are told the Holy Spirit maketh intercession for us with groanings that cannot be uttered. And this is a continuing service, and that, too, is for everybody. In view of these tremendous efforts by each member of the Godhead, does it not seem reasonable to believe that many more than a very small fraction of earth's multitudes will be saved?

We need also to consider what an important part knowledge has in all this. When in agony on the cross, Jesus in his last earnest petition to the Father prayed for those who were engaged in the dastardly task of crucifying Him, "Father, forgive them for they know not what they do." Thus Jesus gave ignorance as a legitimate, or at least pardonable, excuse for wrong doing. But while that might apply to those rough Roman soldiers and to vast numbers who know nothing of Jesus, would it apply to those in our own land who from childhood have had pressed upon them the claims of Jesus? While we must be careful not to give encouragement to anyone to presume upon God's mercy it is a solemn fact that multitudes of our people have but a very inadequate knowledge of the character and work of Jesus, and know nothing of the beauty and satisfaction of a spiritual life.

But there is another passage that must be given very serious consideration.   John 3:36.   "He that believeth on the Son hath everlasting life: and he that believeth not shall not see life."   This and similar passages are so clear and emphatic that there is no occasion for doubt as to their meaning.   However, there is a question as to the meaning of the expression "believeth on the Son."   We are very certain of one thing it does not mean.   It is not simply a matter of words.   Hear the words of Jesus: Matt. 7:22.   "Not everyone that saith unto me, Lord, Lord, shall enter into the Kingdom of Heaven; but he that doeth the will of my Father which is in Heaven."   So the test is doing the will of God.   It is a matter of common knowledge that many people in this land, even in the churches, but very imperfectly know God, and consequently know but little of His will.   And that inevitably means a very faulty service.

There is another factor that needs to be considered in this connection, viz., conscience.   Paul says: Romans 2:14, 15.   "For when the Gentiles (that is heathen) which have not the law do by nature the things contained in the law, these having not the law are a law unto themselves: Which show the work of the law written in their hearts, their conscience also bearing witness, and their thoughts meanwhile accusing or else excusing one another."   No nation, and indeed no normal individual has ever been found without a conscience. This is, I think, clearly one way Jesus has of drawing men unto Himself.   All men have some standards of conduct. Without a knowledge of God the standards are low, and conduct cannot be high. But if anyone makes an honest and earnest effort to be true to the highest and the best that he knows we may be satisfied that our Father will not withhold from him His favor.

God is no respecter of persons, and shows no favoritism. Each individual is judged on his own merits. Jesus stated that Pharisees and lovers of money as classes were usually impenitent because repentance was difficult for them, but that did not mean at all that no Pharisees or rich men would come to Him in the right attitude and be saved. The bigoted Pharisee, Saul of Tarsus, became the great apostle Paul; and Joseph, a rich man, helped to take the body of Jesus from the cross, and tenderly laid it in his own tomb.

It might seem that since each person in the Godhead has endeavored to do everything possible to save everyone that at last there would not be anyone who would finally resist His overtures of mercy. But not so. The two thieves crucified with Him make that clear. One of them acknowledging his guilt seeks help from Jesus and his plea is graciously granted. The other thief in the same condition spurns the glorious opportunity, and thus reveals the gulf that lies between him and Jesus; and he evidently went out into the next world having between him and Jesus a gulf so wide and deep that there could never be over it any passage.

THE DISPENSATION OF THE SON

The next stage is the dispensation of the Son. That is the experience that we speak of when we say being converted, getting religion, professing religion, accept-

ing Christ, or being saved. It is that stage at which we
come to a knowledge of our acceptance with God. How
do we get into this stage from the dispensation of the
Father, or directly from the sinful life?

1. The first step is dissatisfaction with the life as is.

2. A sense of regret for that life, or repentance for
sin.

3. A belief that something better is possible.

4. A willingness to pay the price, (consecration) to
forsake sin.

5. Looking to Jesus in faith.

6. The Consciousness of forgiveness, and the peace
that passeth all understanding.

The realization of this experience may come suddenly or gradually. It may be illustrated by coming to the
light out of darkness. A man is in a dark room, he
turns on an electric switch and the room is immediately flooded with light. Or, as he stands at the window
in the early morning and looks out there is utter darkness. But he may continue to look. From one moment
to another he cannot tell any difference. After sometime, however, the darkness does not seem so intense.
After another period of waiting objects on the outside
may be recognized. Later they become clear, then the
sun arises, and the world and the room become flooded
with light.

Or, to take another figure—a man has on his shoulders a great bag of sand. Its great weight presses down
upon him so heavily that existence is a burden. That
weight may get off in either of two ways: he may throw
it off and at once experience a tremendous relief, or a
hole may be made in the bag and the sand will slowly

and gradually run out.   After awhile it is all out and finally he will realize that the weight is gone.

So it is in the spiritual life.   There may be such dissatisfaction with one's self, such unrest, such a load that seems ever to bear one down that life is a burden. Individual and world problems seethe in his mind and can find no solution.   He often is unable to diagnose his own case.   Finally the knowledge is borne in upon him that what he needs is the shining upon him of God's face.   He turns his helpless hands to God, and expectantly seeks help.   With such an attitude help always comes.   It may come quickly like the flood of electric light or the throwing down a great bag of sand, or it may come so gradually that the exact minute, hour or day may not be known.   But there does come a realization that the darkness is gone, the weight has ceased to bear heavily upon him, life has ceased to be an enigma, and there has come into the heart a sweet peace.

It often happens that a mistake is made by Christian workers in thinking that others must have an experience just like theirs or it is not genuine.   Then, too, seekers of this blessing sometimes think that it must come to them just as it came to some of their friends. We need to be careful not to make either of these mistakes.   There is, however, one inexorable requirement. We must not dictate to God the method, but be willing to do whatever God wants in whatever way He wants.

When one comes into this experience he has reached a higher stage on the stairs that lead to God.   He has the consciousness that his sins have been pardoned, and he can look into the face of God unafraid.   There are four things it does especially: First, it makes one happier. Being in the dispensation of the Father may be sufficient to get us into heaven, but those in it do not have the spiritual satisfaction that those have who have attained to this higher experience. Second, it makes one vastly more useful. One has to get above a low level in order to lift others up. People are pulled not pushed into the higher realms of Christian living. In periods of spiritual awakening great numbers come into this experience. Third, it gives a sense of surety for the future. Those in the dispensation of the Father feel it presumptuous to claim heaven as a certainty. The most they would be able to say would be to express a hope that all will be well in the world beyond the grave. But those in the dispensation of the Son through faith in Him have the privilege of knowing that they have passed from death unto life—not only in this world but if they remain faithful that it will continue in that to come. Fourth, it will greatly enrich our life on the other side. The thief on the cross will enjoy the glories of heaven. But his experience cannot be like that of the Apostle Paul to whom vast multitudes throughout eternity will pay their thributes of praise and gratitude for his heroic life and unselfish service.

THE INTELLECT, THE EMOTIONS, AND THE WILL

Most of the efforts of the Christian Church have seemingly been to get the masses of the world into this stage of spiritual development. The intellect, the emotions, and the will constitute the trio in man that must co-operate in this task. The will must be reached before there is a change of life. But the matter cannot properly be put before the will without the intellect. There must be a background of knowledge for this and every higher experience. The peoples of the world are suffering terribly because they do not know the truth. Then, too, the emotions play an important part. There are some who seem to think that to repress the emotions is an indication of superiority. That is not true at all. Great souls have great emotions. They very properly control them to the extent that they do not make spectacles of themselves in public. But there are occasions when even that may be justified. Jesus, under the stress of the wickedness of Jerusalem cried aloud. Again in the quiet of a little group at the grave of his friend Lazarus the tears of sympathy streamed from his eyes.

Laughter and tears are closely related. There was a tradition that Jesus often cried, but never laughed. It may well be that He never engaged in big ha, ha's. But who is there who can but believe that when He took little children into His arms winsome smiles played upon His lips. George R. Stuart, the beloved evangelist, used to say that he was sure that when God made a monkey and a parrot He knew what they would do and He put the "do" in them. And that He laughed when He did it. There is no necessity for devout Christians to have a lean and hungry look, nor always be weighted down with a serious and solemn expression.

The emotion helps the intellect to move the will. Those who have been bathing in the surf are familiar with the experience of going out a little from the shore and letting the incoming wave gently lift them back to the shore. It is one of the principal delights of sea bathing. The emotion is something like that. A full flood of the emotions co-operating with the intellect arouses the will to action, and charts and directs the life. When that is done a beneficent circle is formed. The intellect is clarified, the valves of the emotion are so opened that the emotional flow is normal, and then in turn the will is fortified. That is to say that the will is not usually reached directly, but through the intellect and the emotions. Now with religious leaders it is a matter of very great importance to learn how best to affect the intellect and the emotions. In the religious life the usual methods of imparting knowledge are employed, especially preaching and Sunday School work. In reaching the emotions these means are used and several others. One almost universal means is music. To such an extent is this true that preaching is practically always accompanied with music. Spiritual hymns especially are themselves a spiritual agency, and in addition they prepare the mind and heart for the message from the preacher. While services on Sundays are important, great spiritual movements have never been brought about by these alone. The great revivals that have swept communities and nations have been brought about by daily meetings lasting for weeks or months, in which preaching, singing, praying, Bible study and personal work would each have a prominent place.

In these meetings effort is made to get the people to yield themselves to God. If they were living in sinful rebellion against God to change completely. If they were living at a low level of religious experience—the dispensation of the Father in the phraseology of this book—they were urged to a higher level, that is to the dispensation of the Son, or having an experience in which there is a certainty of sins forgiven that they may look up into the face of God unafraid. Only occasionally have special efforts been made to get the people to seek and secure the highest religious experience, the dispensation of the Holy Spirit. These revivals have usually centered around some outstanding spiritual leader, as Luther, Calvin, Knox, Wesley, Edwards, Finney, Moody, Evans, Sam Jones, Geo. Stuart, Chapman, Gipsy Smith, Torrey, Billy Sunday, and others not so widely known. But behind these and others who have achieved greatly there have usually been earnest prayer groups.

There has been a disposition among many Church leaders to discredit the accomplishments of revivals. But history will not sustain that position. The nations that have had revivals have had higher standards of morals, and a purer, happier individual, home, and national life than those that have not. Historians agree that England owes much to the Wesleyan revival. The widespread revivals in the United States in the early years of the 19th century unquestionably had the effect of putting America on a vastly higher spiritual level than it had been formerly, and probably the highest that any entire nation has ever had.

DISPENSATION OF THE HOLY SPIRIT

The practical ignoring by the Church in nearly all subsequent ages of one very important event seems almost beyond explanation. I refer to the experience at Pentecost. I do not mean that the historic fact is not known and recognized but its possible significance in the lives of all Christians has seemed in the great majority of cases to be entirely overlooked. When none of his disciples had ever thought of such a thing Jesus foretold it, and told them just what to do till it came. The language that Jesus used with regard to it must have seemed entirely too extravagant and unreasonable. It has certainly been so regarded by most people, saved and unsaved alike, since. In short, Jesus said that experience would mean more to them, would be more valuable to them, than His own presence.

The colossal task of bringing a lost and ruined world to Jesus awaited them, and they were a group of very ordinary folks. They were entirely unfitted to cope with it. Jesus told them so, but they did not need to be told. They felt it. The resurrection helped, of course, but that was not enough. Something else was needed, but what? They did not know. There was only one thing they knew—the only thing anyone ever needs to know with regard to anything—they knew the next step. Jesus had told them to wait as to their public ministry until they received an enduement of power. That they did day by day. They were in constant prayer. The first day, the second day, and on to the ninth day they waited and prayed with no unusual results. The tenth day came, and what a day! The story as told in the second chapter of Acts is familiar to Bible students, but how slow we have been to appreciate its significance, and especially its possibility for us.

Profound changes were effected in the lives of this group of some hundred and twenty men and women.

We are enabled especially to see how it affected Peter. He had been a faithful follower of Jesus for three years. According to the record he was the first to acknowledge Jesus as the Son of God. Surely we can say that He was in the dispensation of the Son. He did believe in Jesus, and loved Him with tender devotion. In return he was dear to Jesus, and was one of three who was closest to Him. And yet in a time of temptation he was so frightened by a servant girl that he even denied that he knew Him. Now, in just a few weeks speaking of Jesus he was so courageous that without hesitation he told the leading Jews to their face before the assembled multitudes, "Him ye have taken and by wicked hands have crucified and slain." A marked change had taken place in Peter. What was it? The name is not nearly so important as the fact. But the name is given. St. Luke called the experience the baptism of the Holy Spirit, and with this experience he and his fellow-workers entered into the dispensation of the Holy Spirit.

There is little disagreement among the followers of our Lord as to the above. But Peter, in this same sermon that so moved the people that about 3000 souls were added to their fellowship, said: "Repent and be baptized, everyone of you in the name of the Lord Jesus for the remission of sins, and ye shall receive the gift of the Holy Ghost. For the promise is unto you, and to your children, and to all that are afar off, even as many as the Lord our God shall call." Everyone of the great multitude to whom he spoke might have this blessed experience, not only so but it would be the privilege of their children and to all that were afar off—in distance or in time. Is not this blessed experience for all of us today who will receive it?

There is an added clause here, "even unto as many as the Lord our God shall call." What does that mean? Does not God call everybody? That He does to some degree there is no doubt, for Jesus said, "And I, if I be lifted above the earth will draw all men unto me." But for this larger blessing it may be said that so far as our knowledge goes those only receive it who have had some previous knowledge of religious truth. But throughout the ages this blessing has come to all conditions of men and women. God here as always is no respecter of persons. The only previous requirement so far as we know is for one to know enough of spiritual things to know about and seek the larger blessing. It must be sought of course in accordance with the conditions, but that being done, God is ready and anxious to pour out His greatest blessings upon the greatest and humblest of men and women alike.

We can perhaps understand this better by looking into the experience of some in modern times who met the conditions and received the blessing of which we speak.

ALDERSGATE TO FETTER LANE

In the foregoing pages consideration has been given to many of the great movements of the world, especially those having to do with moral and spiritual conditions. Some consideration has been given the underlying causes. But this is a matter of such great importance that it would be unfortunate not to give sufficient treatment for a clear understanding of that power that has enabled otherwise ordinary folks to go out and do great things for God and humanity. Impartial historians have given John Wesley credit for having a great part in making this a better world. He had a good intellect that was highly cultivated, but that cannot explain his power. He came to be an effective public speaker, but until he received something else his speaking attracted no attention. He was orderly, and meticulous in details, and a good organizer, but none of these in the early period of his life was a particular asset. But something happened to him. What was it? The explanation usually given is that he had an experience in Aldersgate. One night at a quarter to nine he says his "heart was strangely warmed." This experience should not be treatly lightly. He could now be able to say that Jesus had forgiven his sins. That is a great event in any life. And yet if that had been his only religious experience it is not at all likely that anyone today would know anything about John Wesley except perhaps a few church historians. That he had been in the dispensation of the Father before this seems quite certain. As we consider his fidelity to the highest and the best that he knew it is unthinkable that he had no standing before God at all and that if he had died in that state he would have been cast out forever from the presence of God. We are not sure that he had greater consecration that night or greater faith, but he did have some additional knowledge. A man of very limited education was reading Luther's preface to the Epistle to the Romans, and thus the great reformer through two centuries spoke to the opening heart of the evangelist to be. Wesley had now come into the dispensation of the Son. He now trusted Christ as his Saviour, he did have an assurance of sins forgiven. In spite of the gladness of this new experience there were fluctuations as is nearly always the case in this dispensation.

That very night after he had left the room in Aldersgate Street, he says, "I was much buffeted with temptations, but I cried out and they fled away." They returned again and again. Two days later he describes himself as 'in heaviness through manifold temptations.' Still later he finds a 'want of joy,' and traces its cause to 'want of timely prayer.' In Wesley's experience, in brief, as in the experience of many Christians (in this dispensation) there were fluctuations of spiritual mood. But his experience now had one new feature. While he still had to maintain a daily fight with the forces of evil, he says, "herein I found the difference between this and my former state. Then I was sometimes, if not often, conquered. Now I was always conqueror. Here was struggle, but here, too, was victory."

It was after Aldersgate that he was still convinced that some of the Moravians had an experience that he did not have. It was not long, therefore, until he determined to go to Moravia. Why? It seems perfectly clear that he was still seeking something he did not have. If he had been satisfied that this Aldersgate experience was all that God had for him, all that he needed, all that anybody needed, why did he not go out at once to preaching? Why go on a wild goose chase to Moravia? Can anybody doubt that he went there because his heart bade him do so? He yearned for an experience he did not have, and he thought he might be able to secure it in Moravia. He made the trip.

What did he hear there? It was really a very remarkable story. Here is the story that he must have heard over and over again:

These Moravians were the spiritual descendants of John Huss who for his faith suffered martyrdom some one hundred years before the time of Luther. Through the years in spite of persecution they had been true to the ancient faith.

Although persecution was not so severe at this time as it had been nevertheless there was still much persecution. A young nobleman of Moravia, Count Zinzendorf, who had from early childhood been a very earnest Christian, now as a young man extended a cordial welcome to his own extensive estates to any who were suffering persecution. Considerable numbers came, not only Moravians, but Lutherans, Reformed, Baptists, etc. But they were not all as saintly as we might expect. Questions of predestination, holiness, the meaning and mode of baptism, etc., seemed likely to divide the believers into a number of small and belligerent sects. Then the more earnest and spiritual souls among them began to cry mightily unto the Lord for deliverance. His first answer was a general outpouring upon them of the spirit of grace and supplication. Most of them were very plain people, but their natural leader was Count Zinzendorf. Young, of unusual natural gifts, well educated, with great resources of wealth and position, he was above everything else deeply consecrated to God. In addition to being a man of prayer himself he was active in organizing prayer groups. He drew up a brotherly covenant, calling the disputants "to seek out and emphasize the points upon which they all agreed," rath-

er than stress their differences. Thus a group came to
be of one accord. And they were meeting often to pour
out their hearts in prayer and hymns. This was in
1727. During the summer of that year the interest
gradually deepened until on the 13th of August there
came an outpouring of spiritual power that marked an
epoch in the history of that church, and of the world.
A Moravian historian says:

"Verily the 13th of August was a day of the outpouring of the Holy Spirit. We saw the hand of God and
His wonders, and we were all under the cloud of our
fathers, baptized with their Spirit. The Holy Ghost
came upon us and in those days great signs and wonders took place in our midst.

"Exactly what happened that Wednesday forenoon,
August 13, 1727 in the specially called communion service at Berthelsdorf, none of the participants could
fully describe. They left the house of God that noon
'hardly knowing whether they belonged to earth or had
already gone to heaven.' "

The effects were profound and earth-encircling. It
was a young group that received this wonderful blessing. Count Zinzendorf was only 27, and the average
age of all was probably not above that. From that small
village community during the next twenty-five years
more than one hundred missionaries went out. The
story that follows shows that it was the inspiration
more or less direct of the great evangelistic and missionary movements of the following century.

Can we not in imagination see Wesley as he heard
this story from one and another? It had occurred just
eleven years before this. He now returns to England.

On his return did he go immediately to preaching, and telling about the wonderful blessing he had received at Aldersgate? Evidently not. On the contrary he and a group of like-minded worshippers had frequent prayer meetings, sometimes spending the whole night in prayer. Why these agonizing hours? Does it not seem clear that he was convinced that there was possible a larger religious experience, and his heart was crying out for it? This continued during the closing weeks of 1738.

Reference has been made on previous pages of his next experience, but its importance is such that its repetition in this connection may not seem out of place. On the first day of January, 1739, there were gathered together at a Moravian love feast in Fetter Lane about sixty Moravians, and in addition at least seven Oxford Methodists, all of them ordained clergymen of the Church of England, viz., John and Charles Wesley, George Whitefield, Wesley Hall, Benjamin Ingham, Charles Kinchin, and Richard Hutchins. Of this meeting Wesley wrote: "About three in the morning as we were continuing instant in prayer the power of God came mightily amongst us, insomuch that many cried out for exceeding joy, and many fell to the ground. As soon as we were recovered a little from the awe and amazement at the presence of His Majesty, we broke out with one voice, 'we praise Thee O God, we acknowledge Thee to be the Lord.' "

Before this experience at Fetter Lane John Wesley and his friends had spent much time in prayer. It has been noted that after his experience at Aldersgate he had not been fully satisfied and they had frequent pray-

er meetings extending often far into the night, seeking
for something they did not have. Instead of spending
much time praying for a larger spiritual blessing, the
emphasis now changes and soon they are getting up
early in the morning, even at four o'clock on summer
days, telling the multitudes about the blessings they
had received, blessings that were possible for all who
heard. How similar this story is to the story of Pentecost as related in the second chapter of the Acts of the
Apostles.

How easy it is to quibble about terms! This experience in the language of this book is the dispensation of
the Holy Spirit, or the baptism of the Holy Spirit. Wesley and most of his early followers usually spoke of it
as sanctification. Various other terms are used by different people. The designation is incidental. The experience is the important thing.

See what he says about this more than twenty years
later. On November 1, 1762, he wrote the following to
Messrs. Maxfield, Bell, and Owen: "You have over
and over denied instantaneous sanctification, but I have
known and taught it (and so has my brother as our
writings show) about these twenty years."

To such an extent did he and others of the group of
some sixty persons who received this great blessing on
the first day of January, 1739, preach and testify to this
doctrine that a few years later there were so many who
professed this belief that with his usual painstaking
care he says: "We asked them the most searching questions we could devise. They answered everyone with-

out hesitation and with the utmost simplicity, so that we were fully persuaded that they did not deceive themselves. Not trusting to the testimony of others I carefully examined most of these myself, and in London alone I found six hundred and fifty-two of our Society who were exceeding clear in their experience, and whose testimony I could see no reason to doubt." Mr. Wesley goes on to say that in the case of these with not a single exception they testified that the experience was instantaneous. And he adds that he cannot but believe that this experience is commonly, if not always, an instantaneous work.

Thus, Mr. Wesley is perfectly clear, and no one need have any doubt as to his experience or teaching in the matter. Indeed it is regarded as a fixed Methodist doctrine and experience.

We have been discussing especially the work of the Holy Spirit as it affected groups. The original Pentecost, the wonderful experience in Moravia, and then the outpouring of the Holy Spirit upon Wesley and his friends at Fetter Lane in London. But we must not for a moment think that this great blessing came only to groups. There are innumerable instances when this experience has been enjoyed by individuals under various conditions. Some of these experiences will now be given.

DWIGHT L. MOODY

Let us consider first the experience of the great evangelist, Dwight L. Moody, as told by his son-in-law, Mr. A. P. Pitt. Mr. Moody, starting out as an uneducated boy, was converted and at once became active in religious work. By the time of the great Chicago fire in 1871, he had built up and was pastor of a strong and active church in Chicago. Two faithful and devout women used to attend his meeting and sit on the front seat. He could see by the expression on their faces that they were praying for him, and at the close of the service they would tell him that they were praying for him. They sensed something lacking.

"Praying for him! Why? What for? Wasn't he full of zeal and activity for God? Why didn't they pray for the people?"

"We are praying for you that you may receive the power."

"Haven't I got the power?"

"No, we are praying for you because you need the power of the Holy Spirit."

"I need the power! Why?" said Mr. Moody, speaking of it in after years, "I thought I had power. I had the largest congregation in Chicago, and there were many conversions. I was in a sense satisfied. But right along those godly women kept praying for me, and their earnest talk about anointing for special services set me to thinking. I asked them to come and talk with me, and we got down on our knees. They poured out their hearts that I might receive the filling of the Holy Spirit. There came a great hunger into my soul. I did not know what it was. I began to cry as I never did before. The hunger increased, I really felt that I did not want to live any longer if I could not have this power for service."

Chicago was laid in ashes while he was in this mental and spiritual condition. The great fire commenced on October 8, 1871, and swept out of existence the whole north section of the city where he lived and worked. His church was burnt and his flock was scattered.

Under these circumstances he left for the East to raise money for relief and the wherewithal to build a new church.

Mr. Douglas Russell, an English evangelist, supplies a link here. IIe says he was holding meetings in New York early in 1872 when he heard that Mr. Moody was at work in Brooklyn. Having met and worked with Mr. Moody previously, he crossed to Brooklyn and attended a Bible reading when the subject happened to be "The Holy Spirit: His Person, Office and Work." Asked by Mr. Moody to speak, Mr. Russell made some remarks on Galations 4, saying at one point that all believers have the Spirit of sonship, though all believers do not have the spirit of power for service. Every believer is a child of God, being born of the Holy Spirit, but not every believer has received the filling of the Holy Spirit for service.

At this point Mr. Moody, standing by my side, struck the desk with his fist and exclaimed with vehemence!

"I never saw that before! Been troubled about that for years! Never saw it before."

Mr. Russell says it was the following day, in the streets of New York, that Mr. Moody became conscious of a power coming upon him and flooding his whole being with an overwhelming sense of the love of God in Christ. It was God the Holy Spirit.

Mr. Moody once said that during that trip East the hunger for spiritual power was ever upon him. The

Chicago fire did not dismiss or displace this yearning.

"My heart was not in the work of begging. I could not appeal. I was crying all the time for God to fill me with His Spirit. Well, one day in the city of New York —ah, what a day—I cannot describe it. I seldom refer to it, it is almost too sacred an experience to name. Paul had an experience of which he never spoke for fourteen years. I can only say God revealed Himself to me, and I had such an experience of His love that I had to ask Him to stay His hand. I went to preaching again. The sermons were not different, I did not present any new truth, and yet hundreds were converted. I would not now be placed back where I was before that blessed experience if you should give me the whole world. It would be as the small dust of the balance."

Mr. Moody says further: "This happened years after I was converted. Since then I have never lost the assurance that I am walking in communion with God, and I have a joy in His service that sustains and makes it easy work. I believe I was an older man than I am now; I have been growing younger ever since. I used to be very tired when *preaching three* times a week; now I can preach five times a day and never get tired at all. I have done three times the work I did before, and it gets better every year. It is so easy to do a thing when *love prompts you.* It would be better, it seems to me, to go and break stone than to preach in a professional spirit."

This was the beginning of that larger ministry of Mr. Moody that was felt around the world. It seems to me that no one can read the story and study his life without realizing that there indeed was a Pentecostal outpouring. It was a very definite, positive experience, different from and subsequent to his conversion.

SAM P. JONES

I think most well-informed people will agree that Moody was the greatest spiritual force that America has ever known. Multitudes would place Sam P. Jones next to him in that goodly company. In large sections of the South and West he exerted a spiritual influence that no other man has ever approached. Here follows his own story of the greatest hour of his life:

"Oh, brethren and sisters, you have to turn loose, laying everything on the altar, and sweep out into the ocean of God's infinite love. Thank God, that I ever did that. Some of the sweetest memories of my life and the profoundest experiences of my Christian character are connected with these holiness brethren. Never shall I forget an association with a holiness preacher down in a Georgia town a few years ago. That brother had preached this great blessing with all the earnestness and power of his soul. The tidal wave of salvation was sweeping over the people. He was urging a full and uncompromising consecration of all to God, and that accompanying supreme act of faith which procures the downpour of the Spirit in all His fullness. We were walking alone after one of the services had closed, and turning to me, he said, 'Sam, why in the world, brother, don't you turn loose everything that lies between you and God's fullness and lay hold on this great blessing?' I said, 'Brother P———, everything that stands be-

tween me and my God and the uttermost which He can
do for me is not worth more than a nickel. I wouldn't
give a nickel for anything under the sun that I wouldn't
turn loose in a second that stands between me and
God's fullness.' Brother P——— said, 'Then, Sam you
are just within one nickel of the blessing.' I replied,
'Well, a nickel shan't split such an important matter.'
When I got back to church at the next service the meeting had commenced, and this brother was praying as I
entered the church and knelt down; and he truly had
hold of the horns of the altar. Such praying I never
heard since I was born in the world. The very windows of heaven seemed open. I felt the very presence
of my God; heaven and earth came together. It was a
time of heart-searching, heart-emptying, heart-surren-
dering, and heart-filling. At that meeting, in that
solemn and never-to-be-forgotten hour, I turned loose
the willows that overhung the banks, and swept out
into the very midst of the ocean of God's infinite love,
and the joy of that moment lingers sweetly and inef-
faceably today. Its memory and power have swept
over the lapse of years, and it has been my solace in a
thousand sorrows, my strength in a thousand struggles,
my star of hope through a thousand nights, and like a
sheen of glory will canopy with its light and peace and
triumph my dying hour. Thank God, there is water
enough in the River of Life to cleanse every heart from
all sin."

The experience of these Christian leaders are placed
here prominently because they are so well-known.
There are many others who are scarcely less widely
known, both men and women, of different religious de-

nominations.

John Fletcher was the choice of John Wesley as his successor if Fletcher should outlive him. He believed in this doctrine thoroughly, and testified to it as a personal experience. Very able men believed that he was "the most holy man who has been on this earth since the apostolic age" and yet "he was not so by nature, for he was of a fiery, passionate spirit; insomuch that he had frequently thrown himself upon the floor and lain there most of the night, bathed in tears, imploring victory over his temper."

Miss Frances E. Willard, one of the most widely known, most useful, and best loved women who ever lived has left a ringing testimony. She says, "I cannot describe the deep welling up of joy that gradually passed over me. I was utterly free from care. I was blithe as a bird. The conscious emotional presence of Christ through the Holy Spirit held me. I ran about upon errands just for love," and that feeling and attitude continued through her entire life. She adds, "I am a loyal and orthodox Methodist, but I find good in all religions. No word of faith in God or love to man is alien to my sympathy." Among her last words were, "How beautiful to be with God."

Dr. Lovick Pierce, one of the great preachers of early Methodism, said that for minutes he felt that he could live without breathing, so unutterable was the calm in his soul.

Dr. B. Carradine was pastor of a great church in New Orleans in 1889 when he received this wonderful baptism. He was profoundly stirred, and for years was a powerful preacher emphasizing the possibility

and need of this baptism for everybody. But he felt
constrained to say this: "To lay the emphasis upon the
emotional feature is misleading. It is as unwise here
as it is in conversion to demand certain exalted states
as the criterion in such a case. The instant we make
an overwhelming rapture the standard experience that
instant we grieve and discourage many, and make it
difficult if not impossible for them to secure the longed-
for blessing."

I will mention one other Methodist, James E. School-
field, of Danville, Virginia, of a wealthy Virginia family, who was a very earnest, spiritual and successful lay
evangelist, widely known and greatly beloved. He too
had a wonderful experience, so that he could say:
"From that moment my life was revolutionized."

Though this is a standard Methodist belief, and not
officially accepted by several other denominations as
such, nevertheless, every large denomination and many
small ones have prominent witnesses to the blessedness
of this experience. There is space for only a few:
Madame Guyon of the Catholic Church of whom it was
said that "here was one who in her life shone like a
seraph and obeyed like an angel;" Jonathan Edwards of
the Presbyterian Church, sometimes called "The Isaiah
of the Christian Dispensation," profound wisdom and
seraphic, devotion being so wonderfully united in Him;
Merle D'Aubigne, Lutheran, the exceedingly able and
devout historian of the Reformation.

Charles G. Finney, successively of the Presbyterian
and Congregational churches, had an experience more
like that of St. Paul in that the baptism came so soon
after his conversion. Of his experience Finney said:

"When Christ commsissioned His apostles to preach He told them to abide at Jerusalem till they were endued with power from on high. This power was the baptism of the Holy Ghost poured out upon them. This was an indispensible qualification for success in the ministry."

He was powerfully converted one day out in a patch of woods adjoining the little town where as a young man he was practicing law. That night he was in the back room of his law office. He goes on to say, "There was no light in the room; nevertheless it appeared to me as if it were perfectly light. As I went in (the back room) and shut the door, it seemed as if I met the Lord face to face, as I would see any other man. He said nothing but looked at me in such a manner as to break me down right at His feet. It seemed to me a reality that He stood before me, and I fell down at his feet and poured out my soul to Him. I wept like a child, I bathed his feet with my tears. I received a mighty baptism of the Holy Ghost. Without expecting it, the Holy Spirit descended upon me in a manner that seemed to go through my body and soul."

This man was not only a great revivalist as noted on a previous page, but he was a great educator and author, and was recognized as having one of the keenest intellects of any man of his age.

That distinguished and saintly Baptist missionary, Rev. Dr. Adoniram Judson, says, "Renounce the world, renounce thyself, and flee into His loving arms, which are open to receive thee. Angels will rejoice over thy second conversion, as they did over the first. Thou wilt begin to live in a new world, to breathe a new atmosphere, and behold the light of heaven shining upon thee; and thou wilt begin to love the Lord thy God in a new manner."

Miss Frances Ridley Havergal of the Church of England, author of "Kept For The Master's Use" and other devotional books, says of her experience: "One of the intensest moments of my life was when I saw the force of the word 'cleanseth.' The utterly unexpected and altogether unimagined sense of its fulfillment to me, on simply believing it in its fullness, was just indescribable. I expect nothing like it short of heaven."

The testimony of Mrs. Hannah Whitall Smith, a Quaker, is different from most of those that have been given. We have indicated the probability at least that many have failed to secure this blessing for lack of knowledge. It has been noted that lack of consecration has been the stumbling block in the way of perhaps most who have had good religious advantages. Neither of these seems to have been in her way. But her difficulty seems to have been lack of faith. She says: "I was converted in my twenty-fifth year. My conversion was clear and unmistakable. I knew I was born again, and never from that time have I doubted this." But as time passed her religious life was not satisfactory. "My heart was ill at ease. That I grew in knowledge I could not deny, but neither could I deny that I did not grow in grace. Such was my life; and in spite of much outward earnestness and devotedness, I felt it to be a failure. Often I said to myself that if this was all the gospel Christ had for me, it was a bitterly disappointing thing. I began to long for holiness. I began to groan under the bondage to sin in which I was still held. My whole heart panted after entire conformity to the will of God and unhindered communion with Him. But so thoroughly convinced was I that no efforts or resolutions or prayers of my own would be of any avail, and so ignorant was I of any other way, that I was almost ready to give up in despair. In this time of sore need (1863) God threw into my company some whose experience seemed to be very different from mine. I asked them their secret, and they replied, it was simply ceasing from all efforts of our own and in trusting the Lord to make us holy! Never shall I forget the astonishment this answer gave me. What? I said, do you really mean that you have ceased from your efforts altogether, in your daily living, and that you do nothing but trust the Lord? And does He actually and truly make you conqueror? Like a revelation the glorious possibilities of life such as this flashed upon me, but the idea was too new and wonderful for me to grasp. I had never thought of Christ as being such a Saviour as I now heard Him described to be." The light came to her very gradually and slowly, but it came. She continues: "I trusted Him utterly and entirely. The Lord Jesus Christ became my present Saviour, and my soul found rest at last, such a rest that no words can describe it—rest from all its legal strivings, rest from all its weary conflicts, rest from all its bitter failures. The secret of holiness was revealed to me, and that secret was Christ."

This testimony differs from most others also in the fact that satisfaction came so slowly and gradually. But her after life was such that there was no doubt in her own mind nor in the minds of her friends but that she had received this wonderful blessing. It was this experience that enabled her to write "The Christian's Secret of a Happy Life," a book that has been a blessing to many thousands.

Dr. F. B. Meyer, Baptist preacher of London, early co-worker of Moody, author of some forty books, one of the very greatest preachers of his generation, said that in seeking for a deeper spiritual experience his trouble like that of most people in this country at least was as to consecration. He was afraid God would send him to Africa, and he did not want to go to Africa. While struggling with the question he saw his daughter, a girl of some twelve years, go tripping up the steps of their home. He thought, "What if our little girl should come to her mother and me and say that she expected to do readily just anything we wanted her to do. Would we study and plan to make it hard for her? No, no, we would on the contrary make it just as easy as possible, consistent with the development of her character and future usefulness. And then I thought, will not God be as considerate of me as I am of my child?" He then surrendered his life to God who did not send him to Africa, but gave him a ministry the influence of which extended to Africa and every other continent of the world. Among many others the author of this book was greatly helped by him, both personally and through his books.

One of the most thoroughly consecrated and successful evangelists of today is Rev. Dr. John R. Church. On the 25th anniversary of this experience, he says, "On March 19, 1920, at about one o'clock in the morning God for Christ's sake sanctified my soul by the baptism of the Holy Spirit. I was gloriously converted when I was nine years old. There has never been any doubt in my mind about my conversion. Years later when some friends began to talk to me about the baptism of the Holy Spirit, I felt that I wanted God's best in my life but I did not want to go off into fanaticism. I read my New Testament through eleven times in one month to try to find the teachings of the Bible about the baptism of the Holy Ghost and sanctification, and became convinced that it was the teaching of the Bible. I also read a good deal of Methodist literature and came to see it was one of the greatest doctrines of the Methodist Church.

"I felt the need of something more than I had. I prayed and sought for five months. Then when in a prayer meeting with a group of young college friends the experience came. I shall never forget that night as long as I live. I can't describe the sensation I had when the Holy Spirit came. It seemed to me that streams of living fire swept through my soul and body. This mighty power seemed to sweep back and forth until it seemed that I was being consumed with the fire of the Lord. I felt that if God did not stay His hand I would surely die. When the physical sensation came to an end I had the sweetest peace filling my soul that I have ever known, and I felt that I was as clean and pure as the Spirit of God could make me. I shall never forget that deep sense of cleansing and peace. It is beyond my power to describe it. I felt that my soul was clean and pure not because of any merit of mine, but because of what God had done for me."

Some friends warned him that if he professed and

preached this doctrine, it would ruin him. But today after twenty-five years he is still happy in that experience, and untold thousands revere his name, and rejoice that he ever lived and labored and testified for God, and every year his influence is widening and deepening.

I would mention one other, Rev. Dr. John R. Brooks, a profound Methodist preacher of a generation ago. He wrote a very able book on "Scriptural Sanctification," which unfortunately is now out of print. I was also greatly helped by him personally and through his book.

Just what is accomplished in one who receives this blessing of the Baptism of the Holy Ghost, or sanctification?

There are two very definite results that are brought about by this experience:

1. A cleansing from sin.
2. An empowerment for service.

Some give special emphasis to one of these. Others give greater emphasis to the other.

1. All agree that there is a peace and even an exuberant joy that words cannot express. There is no burden of unforgiven sin. Prayer becomes as natural as breathing because we think of God as a loving Father and we just love to talk to Him.

However, I think that much of the discussion as to whether anyone can sin or does sin after such an experience has been unprofitable. On this point Dr. Asa Mahan, the first President of Oberlin College, said in this connection, "Should I be asked, Have you not sinned during these many years? My reply would be, 'I set up no such pretension as that. This I do profess, however, that I find grace to serve Christ with a pure conscience!"

A great deal depends upon our definition of sin. If we take as our definition of sin, "a conscious and wilful violation of the known will of God," then there have been many who for long periods could claim freedom from sin.

On this point Mr. Wesley said:

"Not only sin, properly so-called, that is, a voluntary transgression of a known law, but sin, improperly so-called, that is, an involuntary transgression of a divine law, known or unknown, needs the atoning blood. I will believe there is no such perfection in this life as excludes involuntary transgressions and mistakes which I apprehend to be naturally consequent on the ignorance and mistakes inseparable from mortality. Therefore, *sinless perfection* is a phrase I never use lest I should seem to contradict myself. I believe a person filled with the love of God is still liable to involuntary transgressions—sins of infirmity."

In general it may be said that the closer we get to God the greater the detestation of sin in our lives, and also that in His presence we will not willingly do that which will grieve Him. It should be noted that the passages in the New Testament with regard to the Baptism of the Holy Spirit do not mention this at all. The Apostle John discusses it but in another connection.

There is another question that is often discussed. Is this experience always instantaneous, and closely allied with it, is it always accompanied with exulting emotion? Nearly all the testimony is in the affirmative to both of these questions. Mr. Wesley states that during a period of forty-five years and after a thorough examination of large numbers, all of them declared their deliverance from sin was instantaneous. He adds, "I cannot but believe that sanctification is commonly, if not always, an instantaneous work."

However, in spite of all this testimony, and my own may be included, I am constrained to believe that this is not as generally true as it seems, that others have received and enjoyed this blessing, but for various reasons have not testified to it. The reason they have not testified to it may be that it came to them so gradually that they considered it simply a larger, fuller experience of the dispensation of the Son, and not a new and special dispensation. I say this for two reasons: First, there is general agreement that in "being saved" or coming into the dispensation of the Son we may come into the experience suddenly, but that also large numbers come in gradually and without great emotion, so that they cannot tell the exact moment or even day or week. Why not the same be true of the larger experience? And this is especially true if the recipient belongs to a denomination that has never accepted this as an article of belief; or in the Methodist Church, if they have never been taught to expect such a blessing. Second, I have known some who have not professed it, but who seemed to me to meet the conditions, especially as to consecration, and who in their lives seemed to show forth the same fruits of the Spirit as are found in those who have had an instantaneous and exultant experience and profess it. I have in mind, for instance, a great Baptist preacher, who, so far as I know, never made any profession of this blessing. Yet, those who had a chance to know him and hear him preach believe that his consecration was full and complete, that whatever God wanted him to do he was ready to undertake. The beauty of his Christian life and his spiritual power are additional reasons for believing that he had a spiritual experience out of the ordinary. Then, too, I have known several others, some prominent, others in the humbler walks of life, who have impressed me the same way.

But, here again we need to remember that the method is incidental. The fact is the important thing. If knowledge, consecration and faith unite there will be a definite and blessed result.

The finest thing is that this sweet and satisfying religious experience is *abiding,* (superior to that of the dispensation of the Son which is subject to lapses). Dr. John R. Brooks says:

"We are profoundly convinced that the believer who has received *the* Baptism of the Holy Ghost realizes such an assurance of divine things as absolutely excludes all doubt of the divinity of Christianity, and his acceptance with God—*such an assurance as expels all doubt of both these facts."* This very clear, positive statement and opinion, I believe is true.

2. It empowers for service. Such is the transforming influence in increasing the usefulness of those who receive this enduement that many people regard this as its main distinction. First of all, it imparts courage. Courage is the rarest of all gifts. Aside from religion some are more richly endowed in this respect than others. But this experience gives a quality of courage that is in addition to and above any natural gift. Import-

ant as it is, however, it must be secondary to the inner experience of peace and purity. God gives an inward peace and purity that transforms the life. But He confers no gifts to be used selfishly. The first gift brings us sweet satisfaction; the second imposes heavy responsibilities. There are a great many very difficult tasks to be done—tasks that may mean struggle and heartache and misunderstanding and long endurance.

These are naturally committed to those who will undertake them, and naturally, too, He commits these tasks to those who have special gifts for their accomplishment.

We might ask what kind of work does this experience fit people for. The answer, though often misunderstood, is very simple—*every kind.* There is a rather general idea that it is largely for two groups, evangelists and reformers. It is probably most apparent in these fields, and doubtless these speak of their experience more readily and more often than do others. But there is no life that it does not elevate; no work that it does not ennoble. A woman so blessed may by the sweetness of her disposition and kindliness of her heart bless a wide community. A man by the purity of his motives and the strength of his determination may give a high moral tone to an extensive section.

In all this we need to remember that life is not a pleasure garden but a battlefield. Bearing this in mind it is easier for us to understand that which perplexes many, viz., why does God permit some of His choicest saints to go through such hard places? In a pleasure garden He would naturally place those near to Him in the most delightful corners; but in a battlefield those on whom He could most surely depend would be placed in the most difficult positions.   But the happy fact in connection with the matter is the conviction that the man with this experience is where God wants him to be, and that he is not alone, but that God is standing by him.   This is one of the great compensations of the fully consecrated life, that God puts him where he is, and therefore it is good.

THE VALUE OF TESTIMONY

The trend of the times is against personal religious testimonies.   If one gives a testimony in Church he often feels under the necessity of accompanying it with an apology.   Paul and other early preachers told their experience over and over again.   This, too, was the practically universal custom of the early Methodist preachers.   The following is an instance where personal testimony had far greater weight than many sermons.

A LAWYER'S TESTIMONY

Some years ago an Annual Methodist Conference was held in a good North Carolina town where some damage to the church made it necessary to hold the services in the County Courthouse.   On Sunday morning before preaching a testimony meeting was held.   At this particular service there was present a citizen from a neighboring town, a very brilliant lawyer in middle life.   But he was dissipated and had come to express atheistic views.   After hearing dozens of testimonies as to the power of God in revolutionizing human lives he said: "I have practiced at this Bar where these testimonies were given for years. Most of these men who testified to the power of God in their life I know personally. Their record for telling the truth is of the very best. I know that many of them made great sacrifices to preach the gospel. I know that if I had a case in court and had one of them as a clear witness for my client I would feel pretty sure of winning my case. If I had two or more so testifying I would feel certain of success. But here it was not one or two or three but dozens of the best men I know all testifying to the same thing. I cannot gainsay their testimony."

In the foregoing pages has been given the testimony to a higher Christian experience of men and women whose names are known among intelligent people throughout the whole world, men and women who by common consent have made by their life and labors this world a better world to live in, and this number might be multiplied indefinitely. Are there those who can still gainsay their testimony?

A COLOSSAL CONFLICT

A Colossal Conflict

There may be some readers who may think that the heading of this chapter is too vigorous for the subject matter. That may be natural because many have never seriously considered how serious some situations have become. We are being forced to know something of the seriousness of war. But most of us have not sufficiently considered that deeds are preceded by and are the result of thoughts. Wars, generally speaking, are a conflict of ideas and of ideals. Other considerations, such as personal ambition, economic welfare, etc., may and usually do enter in, but back of these is the mental and spiritual attitude of the people.

Now, what have the peoples of the world been thinking these last several decades? That is a subject that deserves serious consideration.

There have been throughout the ages many conflicts, in fact it may be said that history is simply a record of the various conflicts of the human mind as translated into action. Two such have been considered specifically in previous pages. One was based on the supposition that Christianity may absorb heathenism without hurt. The result was that the Church became exceedingly corrupt. I was about to say hopelessly corrupt. But that would not be true. Nothing is ever hopeless if Christ is present with any one man to help. It has been said, and truly, that one man with Christ is a majority. There was a serious danger that Christianity would be choked out by heathenism. But Martin Luther was a man that God could use and did use to save the Church.

Then there arose a group of writers who imagined that the world could get along without God, and said so. These men were called deists. Their opinions percolated down through the masses, and moral corruption became common again in the Church, as well as out of it. Deism in large measure was driven out of England by the Wesleyan revival. In America similar influences had to give way, not by any one man, but by quite a number, as indicated in previous pages.

But the great religious movements soon had to meet another foe, different in form, but almost identical in substance. Its general name is modernism. It has had mainly two divisions:

1. Darwinism. In 1859 Darwin published a book, "Origin of Species." His views have been generally considered as one theory, known as evolution. There were in fact two theories. One was probably true, and has been widely accepted as true by scientists. The other has now been determined by research, especially by the Mendelian laws, to be false. It was this false theory that threatened to overturn all former ideas, especially as to the creation of man. Its principal effect was to bring the Bible into disrepute with many as an authoritative source of knowledge.

HIGHER CRITICISM

2. Just a little later Graf, Kuenen, Wellhausen, and others in Germany and surrounding countries in Europe worked out a most ingenious system that

proved to their own satisfaction that the first six books of the Bible were not at all what people have always thought. All the saints and scholars of the past had been mistaken in thinking that these six books were what they appeared to be. But now these bright German professors found out that these books constituted a curious fabrication. They found this out because of the language of the books. These men were gifted students of the Hebrew language which was the language of the Old Testament. For some time there was no clear and convincing answer to these positive speculations. But gradually the spade was doing its work, and during the years a vast amount of writing material has been unearthed which shows that the Bible is right and these bright professors are wrong in many of their leading linguistic assertions. They did not stop with the first six books but went on to overhaul, as it were, the entire Bible.

England, Scotland, and America sent many of their bright young men over to this German group to find out just what parts of the Bible they could not afford to believe, and they returned to teach the rest of us. But the English and American pulpits have been inclined to take a position of compromise. The result has not been paganism such as we see in Germany, but a greatly diluted gospel.

An ambassador delivers the message given him by his sovereign. Any other message is incidental and comparatively worthless. If he has any doubt as to what the message is, his work cannot be very valuable and may be hurtful. The preacher is an ambassador of God. If he has any doubt as to the integrity and authority of God's word he very naturally cannot give an authoritative, "Thus-saith-the-Lord" message. If the Bible does not contain that message, he has no message. If each man may decide for himself just what part is God's message and what is not, then each man makes his own Bible, and the message is his own and not God's. This constitutes the tragedy of modernism.

It may be that there are more of the German people who have not bowed the knee to Baal than we think. The heroic Neimoller and the groups sympathetic with him, and some Catholic groups may be able when the tide of battle turns to present to the world a larger front than now seems possible.

Modernism has been remarkably similar to Arianism and to deism; that is, rationalism against the supernatural. Arianism and deism had as their foundation philosophy; Darwinism, science; higher criticism, mostly history and language. It has been really amazing the way so many religious leaders have accepted these views in all their crudeness. Most of those accepting these conclusions have explained their position by the simple statement that the Bible is not a book of science anyway. And as to higher criticism they explained that the ancients could not be expected to know as much as our modern scholars.

It does not come within the province of this book to discuss these questions in detail. The author of this book has in preparation a volume on that subject. Just here I will say that it was a sad day in the history of the Christian Church when her theological seminaries began to give greater consideration to the half-baked skepticism of some German professors than to the personality and work of the Holy Spirit.

The rationalistic spirit and attitude engendered by the acceptance of these views have been manifested (1) by opposition to revivals; (2) by disbelief in the possibilities of the higher stages of the religious life. A general statement of this fact has been discussed in previous pages. I will here give some illustrations. I will speak especially of the Methodist Church. A similar condition has prevailed in all the larger denominations, but it was more marked in the Methodist Church because belief in holiness and revivals was an integral part of early Methodism. We have seen Mr. Wesley's views on this subject. They are clear-cut and unmistakable. This was true also of the Methodist Church in America. The Episcopal Address of the General Conference of the Methodist Church in 1824, referring to the doctrine of entire sanctification closed with this remarkable statement: "When Methodism forsakes this doctrine, we are a fallen Church."

The Centennial Conference of Methodism, held in Baltimore in December, 1884, and composed of delegates from eight branches of the Methodist family spoke out plainly in its pastoral address. On this subject is the following: "We remind you, brethren, that the mission of Methodism is to promote holiness. Holiness is the fullness of life, the crown of the soul, the joy and strength of the Church. It is not a sentiment nor an emotion, but a principle inwrought in the heart, the culmination of God's work in us, followed by a consecrated life. In all the borders of Methodism the doctrine is preached and the experience of sanctification is urged. We beseech you, brethren, stand by your standards on this subject. Our founders rightly interpreted the mind of the Spirit, and gave us the truth as it is in Jesus. Let us not turn from them to follow strange lights."

This will indicate how faithfully American Methodism was following Mr. Wesley's teaching on the subject.

EXPERIENCE OF GEORGE R. STUART

This continued to be the position of the Church until after Darwinism and higher criticism, "strange lights," had begun to do their deadly work. The changed attitude as to revivals can be seen in the following story concerning an experience of that greatly beloved evangelist, Dr. George R. Stuart, as told by his friend and biographer, Dr. W. W. Pinson, for years Missionary Secretary of the M. E. Church, South:

"During a meeting in Wilmington, N. C., in 1890, Stuart received a telegram from Bishop Keener, who was in charge of the Holston Conference, which read: 'I want you for an important station. Come to the seat of the Conference, Bristol, Tenn., at once.' Stuart read this telegram to Jones. The response was characteristic; 'George, are you going to take your hand off of the throttle of the locomotive engine to roll a wheelbarrow?' Equally characteristic was Stuart's answer: 'I am a member of the Methodist Church. I am a member of the Holston Conference. I agreed to be subject to the laws of my Church. Bishop Keener is in authority. There is nothing left for me but to obey or rebel. I shall take the night train for Bristol.' He tells us that he then walked into his room, laid the telegram on the bed, knelt down, and offered in substance this prayer:

'O Lord, I have surrendered to thee completely and
entirely my life. If I know my own heart, I desire to
go where you want me to go and to do what you want
me to do. Do not suffer me by a changing, vacillating
life to weaken or destroy my life work. If you want me
to devote my time as a soul winner in the evangelistic
work, let me have the authority from thee. If you want
me to give up this work and devote my life to the pastorate, speak so that I may understand. Leave me not
in doubt as to my life work.' This prayer had continued for an hour when Mr. Jones tapped on the door and
said: 'The hour has come for the afternoon service; will
you preach this afternoon?' Stuart replied, 'Yes, this
will be my last sermon.' He walked to the great tabernacle breathing the prayer, 'Speak to thy servant, Lord,
that I may know thy will in this crisis of my life.' He
walked upon the platform and faced five thousand people, took his text and began to preach. Throughout
the whole sermon there was unusual unction and power. People sobbed aloud. 'Amen' and 'Hallelujah'
were heard. In the closing moments of the sermon
there came one of the most marvelous demonstrations
of the Holy Spirit ever witnessed in their great meetings. The pastors of the city were on the platform. Dr.
R. C. Beaman and Dr. W. S. Creasy were the pastors of
the two leading Methodist churches of the city. When
this wonderful demonstration of power came upon the
speaker, these two preachers jumped to their feet at
the same moment and both of them cried 'Hallelujah'
at the very top of their voices. At the same time twenty-five or thirty people all over the audience leaped to
their feet and began to cry aloud and shout. The two

preachers ran across the platform, fell into each other's arms, and people began to shout, embrace each other, and shake hands all over the great audience. At that moment the most marvelous divine touch came upon George Stuart, and he was powerless to speak for a minute. Under this great emotion of the speaker and the audience, the sermon came to a close. The penitents were called and a marvelous spectacle followed—old and young, large and small crowded to the front and fell upon their knees in prayer. It was a service that no one can ever forget who witnessed it. When Mr. Jones and Mr. Stuart returned to their rooms at the hotel, Mr. Stuart said: 'Well, my brother, my life work is settled. God has spoken; let man be silent. I shall tell the bishop my experience. I shall continue my work as an evangelist; but I must obey orders, be loyal to my Church, and report to the Conference, as directed by the bishop.'

"The result was as might have been expected under the circumstances. There had arisen opposition to men who were styled 'roaming evangelists.' Certain of the bishops felt called upon to exercise their authority against members of Annual Conferences being given work that would permit them to travel at large. Sam Jones, for illustration, was given for a time an appointment as agent of the orphanage of his Conference. He finally located, and this put him from under the authority of bishop or conference. The opposition to evangelists became very clamorous at that time. The question became one of such importance as to call for special legislation. It was a dual controversy. It included the doctrine of entire sanctification, or holiness, and of evangelists. They were companion irritants, for the reason that they naturally fell into line with each other. They came to be classed together by the opponents of either, also by the defendants of either. The Church suffered accordingly. This led many leaders in the Church to oppose both. It was discovered that men who did not believe in holiness could make a demonstration by their unholy method of controversy and men professed entire sanctification who made it plain they had been hasty in their profession. In the evangelistic controversy we cooled our fervor and banked our fires. The Church managed to eliminate a lot of its holiness and much of its evangelistic passion.

"George went to the Holston Conference expecting to continue in the evangelistic work, but the bishop stood firm, saying: 'I love George Stuart and shall treat him exactly as I would treat one of my own boys. I need him as pastor and must have him.' Accordingly he was appointed to Centenary Church, at Chattanooga, Tenn. As an obedient son in the Church he accepted the appointment, if not cheerfully at least loyally. The alternative would have been to retire from the traveling connection by voluntary location. This he would not do.

"He preached during that year to great crowds, and his ministry was fruitful. During the year he built a great tabernacle and had his beloved comrade, Sam Jones, come and hold a meeting, which was one of his greatest.

EXPERIENCE OF A METHODIST BISHOP

"At the end of the year strong pressure was brough†

to bear from the churches, civil and social organizations, and practically the entire city to secure his return as pastor. His response was: 'It is the voice of God, not man, that I am heeding. God has spoken. My life work is that of an evangelist.' At the session of Conference he located and rejoined Mr. Jones in the evangelistic work. This continued till the sudden death of Sam Jones in the year 1906."

The changed attitude toward a higher spiritual life developed at the same time as that toward revivals. The following story will give a better idea of the situation than a general statement:

At the turn of the century there was a Methodist Bishop of unusual eloquence and of great spiritual power. I could mention his name but in such reverence do I hold his memory that I would not say anything that might detract an iota from his high standing among all men. He was indeed one of the great preachers of his day and one of the noblest of men. This great man told Dr. John R. Brooks, a good friend, that any man might have the experience of sanctification (or the baptism of the Holy Spirit) if he was willing to pay the price. Now he did not profess to have this experience. His statement could only mean that there was a price he had not been willing to pay. According to the language of this book he belonged in the dispensation of the Son, and in the opinions of those who knew him he had a particularly high place in it. In fact, most people would feel that scarcely any man could have a higher experience. And yet he knew that there was possible for him a higher experience. And he knew there was a price he was not willing to pay. What was that price?

I do not know. But we may say with certainty that it was not of the low or gross order. What could it have been but that it would have been unpopular for him to have and testify to this experience? There had been a time in the Methodist Church when that would have been his greatest glory, but now it would have brought him into a position of disrepute. He personally had probably not been directly affected by the spirit of rationalism, but he was no doubt affected by the pervading influence of it as it existed everywhere about him.

What a power this man might have been if he had had this larger experience! If this great man did not have the courage to oppose the trend of the time, need we be surprised that so few others have done so?

But the need of the human heart is too great for this great blessing to be so encrusted with the conventionality of forms, ceremonies, and perverted opinions as to fail of its purpose. If the larger denominations will not reach out to appropriate the power of God, other denominations will arise that will do so. That, indeed, is what is now taking place.

As the larger denominations began to lose their zeal for evangelism, and to emphasize less and less the personality and work of the Holy Spirit, other small groups were founded to further in whatever way they could this particular work. Many meetings of some of these groups have been such that noise seemed to be one of the main elements of their religion. Then, too, many of the professors of holiness did not exhibit the fruits of righteousness in their lives. Some of these had made profession under undue pressure and without a clear understanding of its meaning. It seems but the truth to say that a few were using these professions to protect their evil doing. But after all allowances have been made it remains true that great numbers have received spiritual blessings that were so pronounced that it may be seen by others in their daily walk and conversation. One rather general criticism of these groups is their disposition to minify the religious experience of those who do not agree with them. But is that weakness confined to these groups?

Of these I mention especially the Church of the Nazarene because they are so much like the early Methodists. They preach sanctification and emphasize evangelistic work just as the Methodists did in their early days. As the early Methodists were, they are also very strict in discipline. They have in their preaching and administration greatly honored the Holy Spirit, and He in turn has greatly honored them. They have as a Church grown very rapidly, and are now established in every state of the Union, in Canada, in Great Britain, and in several foreign fields.

BUD ROBINSON

Their outstanding preacher has been Rev. Bud Robinson, ("Uncle Buddie," as he was affectionately called), a veritable miracle of the grace and power of God. He was born, one of thirteen children, in a hut with a dirt floor in a mountain cove in the East Tennessee mountains. His father was a blockade liquor distiller. Bud's father, brothers, sisters' beaus and others were accustomed to drink, gamble, and fight. Bud was wild, but strange to say he never knew the taste of liquor. In the considerable mountain section where

he lived there were five blockade liquor distilleries,
but no church or school-house. When he was twelve
his father died. Four years later his mother took her
brood of children and her few belongings in a cart
and moved to Texas. He knew as little of Jesus as a
heathen. But a Methodist circuit rider found them and
they went to a nearby camp meeting. He heard in a
sermon something of the life of Jesus which so impressed him that he went out among some of his rough-
neck companions and told them that if any of them
said anything against Jesus he would shoot them. He
evidently thought this had all but recently occurred.
This was the beginning of conviction. He was soon
happily converted. When the preacher announced
that the doors of the Church would be opened he was
perplexed because there was no Church anywhere
about. But he went up with many others. When he
was asked what Church he wanted to join, he said,
"How many do you have?" The preacher told him that
there were four represented there, and he could take
his choice. He then asked the preacher which one he
was in. The preacher told him he was a Methodist, and
Bud said, "I would like for you to put me in that one,"
and that was the way he came to be a Methodist. Many
years later he went over to the Church of the Nazarene.

In addition to his dense ignorance of almost everything, he stammered badly. But he wanted to tell what
great things God had done for him, and began to try
to read. He wanted to preach and applied for license
to exhort. They refused his request. But one of the
committee seeing his earnestness and zeal was somewhat worried and got the others to reconsider. So they

licensed him to exhort with the understanding that he report each quarter. At the end of the quarter he reported that he had preached 90 times and had 90 professions. And there was never any let up. During all this time he spoke on an average at more than 400 public gatherings a year and preached 28,000 times. He went from one side of the continent to the other many times, and it is thought that he preached to a larger number of different audiences than any other man living or dead. The announcement that he was to preach would almost anywhere bring a full house. He wrote much for church papers, and was author of a dozen books.

While still a young man he received an injury which brought him much suffering, and for which they thought there was no remedy. But a Baptist woman who believed in divine healing, and some others prayed for him and he was almost immediately cured. When he was nearly sixty, he was run over by a big automobile and crushed almost to a pulp. Practically every bone of any size in his body was broken. He was rushed to a hospital and laid out for dead. But God raised him up. He lived to be 82, and preached almost to the end. He was not so well known among the intelligentia, but untold thousands of the plain people of America knew him and loved him. He was a man of intellectual vigor and of a fine sense of humor with an interesting lisp (no longer a stammer), but especially he always and everywhere rejoiced to tell what the Holy Spirit can do and does do to help sinning, suffering souls.

Reference was made above to a great man who could not or did not "pay the price." On March 24th, 1942, a man passed from earth to a better world at the age of 85 who could pay the price and did. This world today is a different and better world because he lived and labored and sacrificed. I refer to Dr. Henry Clay Morrison.

Born in Kentucky of good ancestry, when he was two years old his mother died. Two years later his father died. His grandfather gave him a happy home until his death. Then for some years in the difficult days following the war between the States he had to make his own way, working for quite a while as farm laborer, during which period he built up a strong physique that stood him in good stead for many years of strenuous labor. He had very limited school advantages, but profited from what he had, and especially from a debating society in which he took an active part.

While still in the home of his grandfather he was converted in a Methodist Church, and his conversion was so clear and satisfying that long after he said: "Many years of conflict have passed since that glad night, but sitting here in the silent room, by the smouldering fire in the grate, the memory of the incidents of that happy hour are as clear and fresh in my mind as if they had all occurred only last week."

His call to the ministry was likewise clear and positive. The pastor and several other friends were kind and helpful. Though hardly more than a boy he was soon a junior preacher on a circuit. His earnestness,

his friendliness and his unusual eloquence were such
that from the beginning he had good audiences. He
was a thinker and a student as well as a born orator,
and it was not long until he was filling some of the better appointments. He then took a year off to study in
the theological department of Vanderbilt University.
On his return to the pastorate the leading places were
open to him. He was particularly fond of evangelistic
work, and in his own and in other charges he conducted
successful revival meetings.

Now when everything seemed so satisfactory in his
work, with most brilliant prospects for the future he
had times of sore heart hunger, an impetuous temper, a
lack of peace and abiding power. One of his friends
had entered into the experience of holiness, and that
concentrated his thinking on that subject until he became convinced that that experience was what he needed. The feeling became so unbearable that he sought
the advice and counsel of Dr. McKee, a scholarly and
saintly Presbyterian preacher and theological professor
who had some years before received the same experience. "My young brother," he said, "the Lord has not
forsaken you, but is leading you into what Mr. Wesley
called 'Christian perfection,' the Baptists call it 'rest of
faith,' the Presbyterians call it 'the higher life,' or 'the
fullness of the Spirit.'" The floodgates broke in upon
his soul, but the fear of what his cultured and fastidious
congregation might think of his profession of sanctification checked the Spirit's work. Heart-searching days
followed. There lay before him a brilliant future.
Large, cultured city churches were available to him. In
a few years the bishopric seemed practically certain.

During these days he settled the question and determined at whatever cost to pay the price. Of this experience his biographer, Dr. C. F. Wimberly, says:

"Henry Morrison, however, became fully rooted
and grounded in this Great Depositum of Methodism,
as many parts of the world have found out. It was this
soul revolution which cast out, and cast off, all social
and ecclesiastical autocracy; it marked the Independence Day of this chosen vessel; it was the crossing over
day of Jordan into the Canaan of peace, joy, persecution—and Power. The door was effectually opened, but
there were many adversaries. Once Morrison became
established, faces of clay, social and religious prefer-
ment, the tongue of criticism and ridicule were unable
to move him. The needle was never truer to the pole
than he has been to this great truth, and as a result, for
every door that was closed through prejudice and misunderstanding, God has opened for him hundreds of
others; so that his lines have gone out in all the earth
declaring to rich and poor, high and low, in cathedrals
and brush-arbors, conferences and camp meetings, that
God can save and sanctify the soul of every believer,
through the merits of Jesus' blood—all men, everywhere."

So successful had he been in revival work that many
calls came to him from other pastors, calls which in
most cases he could not accept. There had been growing in him the conviction that he should give his entire
time to it. Most of his friends tried to dissuade him as
the field of independent evangelism at that time was
unpopular. But he became convinced that this was his
duty—so at the end of the second year of a notably suc-

cessful pastorate at Frankfort, the state capital, he resigned the pastorate to take up the new work. That which troubled him most was that the field was white unto the harvest, and he could do so little, even though there was a constant strain of overwork. He was especially troubled because of the serious falling away from the great fundamentals of Methodism, the Methodist Press in Kentucky being among the worst offenders.

Now a great need meant a new call—a call to use the printed as well as the spoken word. He had no money but on faith he projected a little four-page monthly sheet to help meet the needs of the situation. There were many who had no sympathy with his purpose nor faith in his methods, and these predicted that there would be soon a journalistic death, and a funeral without honor. But contrary to their expectations and wishes it became a weekly and larger. He did most of the editorial and other writing in connection with his evangelistic work. But the finances were a constant strain. He mortgaged his home to get money. Once the paper house gave his account to a lawyer to collect and a foreclosure threatened. But he won out in such manner that the influence of The Pentecostal Herald became world wide.

In the meantime the sentiment among many church leaders against evangelists and what most of them stood for had become so pronounced that legislation was passed giving the pastors and presiding elders power to prevent any Methodist Evangelist from going into their territory without their permission. He was invited to preach at a camp meeting in Texas. The Methodist Church authorities in that section objected, but he

felt they had no authority in that case and he went anyway. The result was that he was actually expelled
from the membership and ministry of the Methodist
Church. But instead of hurting it helped him. There
was a greatly increased demand for his services, and
new subscriptions poured into The Pentecostal Herald.
His opponents came to realize that they had committed
not only a crime, but a blunder, and had the whole
transaction expunged from the record.

When it seemed that the academic world had very
generally accepted the modernistic viewpoint a small
group founded a college in Wilmore, Kentucky, to be
faithful to the beliefs, principles, and practices of early
Methodism, and named it Asbury, after America's first
great bishop. In a very limited way it did a valuable
work. But an important building was burned, they
had no endowment, and were in debt besides, and it
seemed that the property would have to be sold to pay
their debts. In their perplexity the Board of Trustees
unanimously agreed that there was only one man who
could save the institution, Dr. H. C. Morrison. They
laid the urgency of the situation before him. It seemed
such a clear call that he could not refuse. There is no
need for details. The fact is that he built a great "A"
grade college on not a narrow but a broad spiritual
foundation, and he did this in addition to, or rather in
connection with his evangelistic and editorial work.
And in addition to this he wrote a number of books
that had a large sale.

In his later years he was much honored and his
great worth widely appreciated. He was guest speaker
at many Annual Conferences, and brought messages

such as only one of such deep consecration, unusual experience, and matchless oratory could bring. He did more than any other man of his time to check the destructive trend to modernism. There follow some excerpts from a recent tribute by Bishop Arthur J. Moore, an intimate friend:

"For nearly thirty years I enjoyed intimate association with Doctor Morrison. The difference in age never seemed to become a barrier to our friendship. His interests were varied, his talents were many, his aim was single. The Christian pulpit was his throne. To the high calling of the ministry he gave himself with singleness of purpose. He had extraordinary ability in leading men into the knowledge of God's redeeming power and to inspire in them loyalty to the principles of Christian living. He was a spiritual and intellectual genius. No one who knew him could doubt the sincerity and the simplicity of his piety. Christ was a very real and present person to him, and he lived in the consciousness of vital fellowship with the living God.

"Dr. Morrison was throughout his life an evangelical and evangelistic preacher. He carried about him a sense of the divine presence; divine power endued him; the eternal voice speaking through him made him indeed one of the prophets of God. His preaching convinced the mind, convicted the conscience and compelled the will. He brought home to men a sense of the eternal and the invisible. He might have said of himself without irreverence, 'I am come that they might have life, and have it more abundantly.'

"He was a tireless worker. Since I first knew him he has carried the duties and the responsibilities of at least three busy men. As editor of The Pentecostal Herald, as builder, friend and sometimes president of Asbury College, and Seminary, as an evangelist with a nation-wide ministry, he gave himself without reservation to the performance of these duties. Yet he found time for his friends and occasionally for a brief season of relaxation for body and mind. Some of my loveliest memories of Dr. Morrison are associated with these days of rest in God's great out of doors.

"No man could know him and doubt his sincerity. There was nothing artificial about him and he wasted no time on non-essentials; Christianity for him was infinitely more than a ceremony. It was a life to be lived, an experience to be enjoyed, a message to be preached, a kingdom to be built. He had but one work and that was to preach Christ. His sane judgment, his dominating conscience, his strong faith were all instruments to be used for the glory of God and the salvation of men.

"He was by nature a warrior. His intense convictions, his fiery earnestness, his dramatic and oratorical ability were all powers which he used to turn back the forces of wickedness and make Christ the master of men. He had thought his way through to some great convictions and he stood ready to defend those convictions against all opposition. While always ready to defend the faith once delivered to the saints his passion was not to defend but to promote Christianity. However, he stood against every effort to compromise Christianity. He was the unrelenting foe of low ideals, comfortable and complacent attitudes.

"I shall always remember the following excellencies

which were so evident in him: First, his overmastering sense of God's presence and power. Second, his intimate fellowship with Christ as his Saviour. Third, his abiding consciousness of full pardon and complete cleansing from all sin through the shed blood of Christ. Fourth, the inner victory and outward success which were his through the baptism of the Holy Spirit. Fifth, his ability to live conspicuously for the unseen. Sixth, the transparency of his sincerity, Seventh, his indefatigable labors for the salvation of men. Eighth, the spontaneity of his humor. Ninth, his chivalry toward women and children. Tenth, the clearness of his vision and the strength of his courage.

"Throughout his lifetime he was the exponent and champion of the Wesleyan doctrine of entire sanctification as a second work of grace. He not only proclaimed but exhibited in his life the doctrine of perfect love. To him, more than to any other one man, we are indebted for keeping this original standard of Methodism alive in the modern church. There was a time when controversy surrounded the proclamation of this message, but during the last thirty or more years of his life the general and annual conferences, as well as many of the leading churches of the nation, have eagerly sought his presence and waited for this message. All the magnificent powers of his intellect and soul were used in the presentation of his experience to those who heard him. Everything else was subsidiary and comparatively insignificant. Because of the faithfulness of this man Methodism is infinitely richer.

"It is hard to think of his exit from our earthly scene, but he will be much at home in the heavenly company. It is inconceivable that the grave should be the finish of a life like his. He is this morning in full possession of his faculties standing in God's presence, feeling in every fibre of his being the immortal life which Christ gives to those who love and serve him."

DR. MORRISON PAID THE PRICE

In imagination I see on the other side a vast multitude in white robes. Who are they? These are they who have been brought directly or indirectly by Dr. Morrison to the Fount of Calvary, and have had their robes washed and made white in the blood of the Lamb.

Was the price Dr. Morrison paid too high?

THE WORLD'S GREATEST TRAGEDY

I once knew a man whose many excellent qualities were marred by the use of strong drink. When urged to take treatment at the Keeley Institute he said, "No, that would not suit me. I don't want to be a drunkard and get down in the gutter. But Keeley will take away the taste for liquor, and I don't want that done. What I want is just a half-a-cure." Does not that statement cover a far wider range than whiskey drinking? Who is it that wants to lie as a drunkard in the gutter? Who is it that doesn't revolt at the idea of being a moral leper? Who can envy the lot of a miser? Who wants the reputation of being a notorious liar? These conditions do not attract but repel. But is not the desire for just a half-a-cure more far-reaching than the drinker threatened with the gutter? Is it not true that this is what the multitudes of earth want for their sin-cursed souls? Is is not true beyond understanding that even preachers and other Christian workers will earnestly plead with sinners to yield their lives to Jesus, that is, to come into the dispensation of the Son, while they themselves by failure to make a complete surrender to God are refusing to come into the dispensation of the Holy Ghost?

Seeing the vast possibilities for increased happiness and usefulness in this larger experience, and in view of the fact, that so many are willing to live on such a low spiritual level, and are often somewhat peeved if urged to go up higher in the spiritual realm, and of the further fact that they are so well satisfied with half-a-cure, and indeed, that this constitutes their ideal and goal, may we not conclude that this is the greatest tragedy in the world? Do we not have reason to believe, too, that this is evidence of an inherited taint of sin just as surely as are the lowest stages of spiritual degradation?

RELIGIOUS CONDITIONS TODAY

The atomic bomb startled the world. Though it has not made the people of the world religious, it has showed them that religion is the one thing the world needs above all others.

"I am a member of the League of Frightened Men. I am literally scared to death. We have walked right up to it. Either the world accepts the Christian way of life, or we are sunk." These are the words of Bruce Thomas, a well-known lecturer and free-lance correspondent who has been around the world numerous times. Substantially the same thing is being said by many thoughtful men.

There are always plenty of pessimists who can see only the gloomy side of life, but this is no ordinary note of pessimism. It is a matter of generally accepted fact that the moral and spiritual condition of the world is distressingly low. If proof were needed it is all about us.

This country spent last year for alcoholic beverages over eight billion dollars, eight times as much as for religion. And women drinkers are getting to be almost as serious a problem as that of men.

Juvenile delinquency—and that usually means adult delinquency as well—is at an all-time high.

Sunday School and Church attendance has been steadily falling off for a generation. In England, it is stated on what seems reliable authority, that not more than ten per cent of the people attend church except on special occasions, such as Easter, funerals, etc.

Approximately a third of the marriages end in divorce.

Christ's last command was, "Go ye into all the world," etc. Some of the largest denominations are averaging only around one cent a week per member for this purpose. Yet, every man, woman, and child average one dollar a week each for alcoholic beverages.

This list might be continued almost indefinitely, but it is not necessary. The important thing is, what is the cause and the cure? There is no single cause except the natural waywardness of the human heart. But we know there is a connection between belief and action. When we cease to think that the Bible is an absolutely reliable message from God, and when we cease to think that Jesus is God, and that through His death we may have forgiveness of our sins, then we are adrift in an ocean of doubt, with no compass and no rudder. And there has been a vast change in the thinking of the people, beginning in the later years of the last century and continuing until today. Darwinian evolution and what is known as higher criticism are having their deadening effect.

For multitudes the Bible is no longer an authority. This is true to a very large extent of the academic world, including even many of our theological seminaries. Many of these institutions, built and endowed by the sacrifices of godly men and women, now have teachers not only lacking that spiritual fervor that characterized many of our teachers of an earlier period, but many are irreligious, and some are even atheistic. Disbelief in the Old Testament and in the Virgin birth is common. Dr. Dan Poling, editor of the Christian Herald, some months ago stated that he had it on good authority that the president of one of the oldest theological seminaries of the country stated before about a hundred preachers that he no longer believed in the historicity of the resurrection. Young preachers coming from such an institution can scarcely be expected to speak with authority, and in fact, do not. Their diction may be beautiful, their rhetoric without a flaw, but if they are not trustworthy ambassadors for God, their message cannot be the means of lifting men to God.

The morals of our people are not so bad as they were in the later years of deism. Especially is that true of the ministry. The morals of our preachers are almost altogether above reproach, and of course many —we hope most—are preaching spiritual sermons; but the spiritual unbelief prevailing makes it difficult to secure spiritual results.

But let us not forget this: the Bible is a supernatural book. Christianity is a supernatural religion. Or

both together constitute the most colossal fraud the
world has ever known.

There is one thing that would be provoking to conservatives, if they would only deign to take it seriously;
it is the arrogant way in which liberals lay claim to
superior scholarship. There was a short period when
there seemed to some a justification for such a claim.
That was because the liberal views were new and
strange, and naturally attracted attention; and especially because it suited those who were seeking an excuse for not accepting the supernatural. But it was not
long until conservative scholarship showed the errors
of the liberal claims.

Liberals have vaunted the names of Darwin, Graf,
Kuenen, and Wellhausen.. Conservatives place against
Darwin, whose views are accepted as hypotheses,
Gregor Mendel, whose views are accepted as laws—and
accepted just as freely as the laws of gravitation. Ju-
lius Wellhausen, the acknowledged leader in higher
criticism, was absolutely opposed by Robert Dick Wilson, probably the greatest linguist that ever lived. He
was a better and more dependable student of Hebrew
than Wellhausen, because, coming later, the spade had
put at his disposal a great mass of material of the Biblical period that Wellhausen· did not have. Therefore,
Wilson could correct the errors of Wellhausen.

Another great conservative who has been dead
some years was Dr. A. C. Dixon, pastor for some time
of Spurgeon's great tabernacle in London. According
to Dr. F. B. Meyer, another great Baptist preacher of
London, Dr. Dixon was the only man after Spurgeon
who had ever been able to draw congregations to fill

the tabernacle. Dr. Dixon was one of the first men to realize the seriousness of the struggle into which we were entering, especially as he had seen what it had already begun to mean in England and Scotland. It was for that reason that he inspired and edited a series of booklets called "The Fundamentals," that were sent free to a great many preachers and other religious leaders a generation ago. This was financed by two laymen. Dr. Dixon was also pastor of several large churches in America. He died suddenly, in his prime.

For a good many years the liberals took the initiative, and the conservatives were on the defensive. Now that situation is being reversed. The conservatives are taking the offensive, and the liberals are thus forced to take the defensive. Today there are three outstanding conservatives, each with a large and increasingly vocal following. Rev. Bob Shuler, who is pastor of a very large church in Los Angeles, has for several years been a fighter for right thinking and right action. He publishes a monthly paper called "The Methodist Challenge." He spoke over the radio, and helped greatly in fighting corruption in his city. But the religious modernists and corrupt politicians and grafters succeeded in putting him off the air. But they cannot stop the printed page, nor his pulpit voice, because his great church is solidly behind him and his two able preacher sons.

Another man notable for his work in this field, is Rev. Walter Maier, a Lutheran of St. Louis. It is estimated by radio authorities that some ten million people listen to his weekly broadcasts. This is by far the largest number who has ever listened to any regular broadcast. The interest maintained over a long period and the readiness with which the great expenses are met for these thoroughly evangelical and anti-modernist messages, give some indication as to what the masses of our people are interested in.

But the most vigorous opponent of modernism that has yet appeared is a comparatively young man, Rev. Carl McIntyre, of Collingswood, N. J. Because he and others likeminded refused to support some enterprises of the Northern Presbyterian Church on account of their modernism, they were expelled from the membership and ministry of the church. They promptly founded a new denomination, the Bible Presbyterian Church. He is now pastor of a large church in Collingswood. He also edits a weekly paper, "The Christian Beacon," and is author of several books. Together with others, he organized the American Council of Christian Churches, which very strongly opposes many of the activities of the Federal Council of Churches. One of his books, "The Twentieth Century Reformation," boldly attacks the beliefs and activities of many men prominent in the religious world.

It is easy to see that modernists would bitterly oppose these men. It is not so easy to understand why they are opposed by those who are sound in their belief in the Bible. But the contest is now on. The differences between the different denominations no longer appear important. The difference now is within the churches. It is a contest between those who believe the Bible and those who believe it in spots, and each man selects the special spots that appeal to him and rejects those that do not. That is, the contest is between the conservatives and the liberals. It is most intense just now in the Southern Presbyterian Church. The issue is as to union with the Northern Presbyterian Church. Most of the older ministers oppose it because they think modernism is worse in the Northern Church. Most of the younger men, recently from the seminaries, favor it. Many of the laymen are opposing some of the things that the Federal Council is sponsoring, such as the effort to replace the profit motive with some sort of collectivism, and are insisting that the Southern Presbyterian Church withdraw from that body.

The low spiritual state of the world, we may confidently say, will not continue. But how will it be changed? Dr. Shuler believes that Methodists should stay in the Church and fight modernism face to face. Dr. Maier believes the Lutherans should do likewise. But Carl McIntyre believes that the present great church organizations are hopelessly modernistic, and that it is necessary for the conservatives to withdraw, and to fight unhampered by the pressure of the great organizations. His slogan is, "Come out from among them and be ye separate." There are others who believe that the hope of the world lies in new, small churches, such as The Nazarene, The Church of God, the Wesleyan Methodists, The Youth Movement, Independent Baptists, the Bible Presbyterians, etc. They remember that the early Methodists were held in very light esteem, but that it was the beginning of the great spiritual movement that in large measure saved the world from the incubus of deism.

But whatever forms the organizations may take, one thing is vital and necessary—there must go up to God

from individuals and groups earnest prayer to God for
the Holy Spirit's presence and power in the hearts of
world-weary men and women.

A good many years ago I went to my mother's home
in the country. A great snow storm came, probably
the greatest I have ever known, and it was terribly
cold, the thermometer for days hovering around zero.
I remember looking out the window at the vast mass of
snow on field and forest, and the question arose in my
mind if human power and ingenuity could remove this
terrible incubus from the earth, if human organization
could gather wood and coal and melt it, and change the
freezing atmosphere so that animal life might have
comfort, and flowers and fruits come again.

The very idea, of course, was more fanciful than a
fairy tale. But something remarkable did occur. After
some days, the warm rays of the sun began to pierce
through the clouds, the snow melted away, and in due
time we rejoiced again in seed time and harvest.

We look today upon a world upon which is spread
out the fearful incubus of modernism. The spiritual atmosphere is distressingly low. What can be done about
it? Can human forces be so organized that the atmosphere shall be changed, and fruitful spiritual harvests
come again—nay, nay, no more than that human forces
could remove the snow. But, thank God, we are not
helpless and hopeless. The Holy Spirit can pierce the
clouds of doubt and despair and bring again to a troubled world the assurance of His presence and power.
What we need to do is to bow humbly and helplessly
before Him, and seek His guidance into the larger life
that is possible for us as individuals and nations.

Stating again very briefly the views of the foregoing pages: Every infant is in the dispensation of the Father. As he comes to years of accountability, he may rebel against God, he may remain in the dispensation of the Father, or he may advance by faith into the dispensation of the Son. To remain in the dispensation of the Father, there must be in him a determination to make an earnest and honest effort to be true to the highest and the best that he knows. As he comes to find that there is something better, he finds that he may have an assurance of the fact that his sins are forgiven, and that he may have a peace that he has not hitherto known. This comes not by works, but by faith, and is for everybody who will look up in faith to God and receive it. Unfortunately, many people think that this represents the high water mark of Christian experience in this world, that we need not hope for or expect anything better until we pass over into a better world. But there have been given the experiences of men and women of such standing that their testimony cannot be denied nor ignored. The number of these witnesses might be multiplied a thousand fold. That testimony is, that after coming into the dispensation of the Son, an experience that we usually speak of as conversion, it is possible for us to enter into a higher dispensation, that of the Holy Spirit, or sanctification. This comes from fuller knowledge, a larger faith, and especially with a complete consecration to the will of God. In this dispensation there is a sweet and satisfying experience, and a courage to undertake and carry forward any work the Holy Spirit may have for us to do.

There was traced briefly a history of the Christian Church, its rapid expansion and the corruption that followed, the reformation by Luther by which Western Christendom was separated into two divisions—those who protested and finally came out as Protestants, and those who remained in the Catholic Church.

It was noted that throughout the centuries there have from time to time been serious struggles of rationalism against the supernatural. In the early Church Arianism greatly retarded spiritual development. In Protestantism two widely diffused developments of rationalism, deism and modernism, have tremendously hindered the development of the Christian Church. Germany has been the leader and principal sponsor of modernism which has been and is the great curse of our time. Its evil effects have been especially seen in its opposition to evangelism and the higher stages of Christian experience. Its evil effects, however, are also seen everywhere about us, and we are beginning rather slowly to realize that this is responsible for much of the evil with which our world is now inundated.

A PERSONAL EXPERIENCE

I would not think of writing this book but for the fact of my own experience. As indicated in the cases of others mentioned in previous pages one very naturally hesitates to parade before the world some of the deeper experiences of his life. But we are to testify to the truth as we experience it, so I shall speak briefly of my experience.

I cannot remember the time when I did not feel called to preach and never kicked against it. I am thoroughly convinced that during that experience I was in the dispensation of the Father. I was never consciously rebellious against God. My sins troubled me and I was repentant and there was much fear in my life. Then as a lad of fourteen I made a profession and joined the Church. This was not sudden, but within some two weeks a change was wrought in me, that satisfied me of my acceptance with God, and that gave me a peace that made life sweet and happy. This experience lasted for several years. During that period I never doubted my acceptance with God, and my experience generally was happy, because there was peace in my heart. In my early manhood I came in close touch with Dr. John P. Brooks, and from him received first-hand knowledge of this larger blessing and I read a considerable part of his large library on the subject. As is nearly always the case of anyone who will consider the subject with an open mind I came to believe that there was such a blessing, and then that I wanted it.

In the meantime I had taken a position as pastor of a little mission Church in a cotton mill district, as I thought, just for a few months. Conditions were bad. The hours were long, they were working a day shift and a night shift. Little children were working long hours. There was an immense amount of moving. One house in some cases would have several different families during the year, and only a small proportion stayed through an entire year. There were open bars and much drinking and drunkenness. I became impressed that I should write and let the world know the situation. I visited my mother's family and told them I thought of writing. They advised me not to do it, as it would make people mad and do no good. They said let older and more prominent men do it. But older and more prominent men did not seem to know or care very much about it. One day soon after this, I was on an elevation looking over the scene, thinking of the situation, and the question came to me—not audibly, but forcefully, "What sort of preacher do you expect to be —say what you think you ought to, or try to be popular?" That settled it. I said, "I will write." I was scheduled soon for a paper to the interdenominational preachers' meeting of the city, of which I was at the time secretary. I spent a good deal of time assembling material and writing a rather long article. They ordered it published in the daily paper, which was done. It occasioned not a little comment, both favorable and unfavorable. But I had kept faith with my own soul. About two months later our Annual Conference was in session in Winston. Bishop Fitzgerald was preaching Sunday morning on "The Holy Spirit." There came upon me a feeling of inexpressible happiness. Tears streamed from my eyes, and my heart seemed overflowing with love to everybody, and with a joy unspeakable. I was reporting the Conference for the daily paper, but for sometime I could not write. When I could there were no adjectives sufficient to tell the story. I thought everybody was affected as I was. I evidently found some adjectives, though, for while the paper ordinarily used my copy just as I submitted it, this time the editor greatly modified my extravagant statements. After getting out I found that others were not so impressed. After thinking over it I became thoroughly satisfied that this experience was nothing less than the baptism of the Holy Spirit nor have I ever doubted it since. I am satisfied that I made it possible for God to so bless me when I determined to do what I felt I should do regardless of consequences.

Within a few months I felt called to undertake a task of unusual difficulty. Nearly all my friends advised against it. But for this experience I would have never had the courage to do it. But there was only one question, "Did God want me to do it?" That became clear to me and I did it. Years later I felt impelled to undertake another difficult task, and again I had very little encouragement from others. There have been difficulties and struggles a plenty, but there has never been a time when I did not feel the conscious presence and guidance of the Holy Spirit. I have been positive and determined, and He has had to check me many times. Most of the time I have seen later that His way was better than what I had planned, and was able to thank Him for changing my course.

What has it meant to me? Much more than I can say. This I may simply say after many checkered years: I would not exchange this experience for all the wealth and glory of the world.

In the following pages are some practical comments about experiences of our everyday life that may reasonably be inferred from the conclusions herein reached.

ILLUSTRATIVE COMMENTS

Illustrative Comments

There is a widely prevalent view that work is a curse; that those people are to be envied who have such accumulated wealth that they do not have to work; that women who can spend all their time going from beauty parlors and dress makers to entertainments are the elite of the earth; that men who can turn over the irksome details of their business to managers while they seek diversion wherever it may be found are fortune's favorites.

But actual conditions reveal the fact that this is not true. Only those are happy for long whose minds are actively employed in some worthwhile task. It is only by activity that the best in life may be developed.

I stood one day at a lumber mill at which some workmen were operating a great turning lathe. They brought to it a large pine log, crooked, and gnarled, and it was tightly clasped at each end so it could turn easily. Sharp knives were so placed that as the log turned rapidly there could be chipped off the protruding parts. As the process continued the knives were pushed closer and closer to the heart of the log until it was being cut at every point, and there was produced a beautiful, symmetrical column that a little later graced a magnificent building. For this unshapely log to be converted into a beautiful column two things were necessary: The log had to be kept in motion, and the protruding parts had to be cut off by sharp knives. How like that is the development of human character? Even God cannot develop a man who refuses to move, and in the development of the finest character it is usually necessary for the sharp knives of difficulty, struggle, and affliction to cut out the ugly things of life and give opportunity instead for the development of the noble and beautiful.

I desire here to discuss just one phase of the subject. It is the matter simply of working against God, or working together with God. It is easy enough to find misery in a palace, and happiness in a cottage. The reverse may also be true. Happiness does not inhere in the palace or in the cottage, but in the human heart. God thinks too much of man to let him find satisfaction in a heart of rebellion. A sinner may have worldly success but not inward peace. In the dispensation of the Father he is not fighting against God, but there is usually no feeling of comradeship. In the dispensation of the Son the outlook is different. He feels that God is his friend and helper. He feels that he has a right to go to God for help in time of difficulty, and not be disappointed. At times there is an overwhelming sense of God's presence. At other times God seems so far away that man wonders whether God hears his cry or not. In the dispensation of the Spirit it is like being in a different world. In every place and at every moment because he has absolutely and unconditionally given his life to the guidance of the Holy Spirit he is conscious of divine guidance. It matters not how hard the conditions he is sustained by the fact that he is helping God do His work. He knows that it is an enormous job to lift humanity out of ignorance and sin, and he rejoices that he can help God accomplish the task. He has the conviction that he has yielded himself to the guidance of the Holy Spirit and he is just where God wants him to be and doing what God wants him to do.

MISSIONS

The viewpoint of foreign missions is undergoing numerous changes. This has indeed been going on for a number of years, but since the first World War the change has been very noticeable. The general viewpoint in all the earlier years was that we were altogether right and the people of the heathen nations were altogether wrong. That was not only the view held here at home, but was the view that the missionaries usually took with them. But the more thoughtful missionaries gradually were forced to modify their opinions. For in the land of heathenism there were those who according to their light were living blameless and even noble lives. But their light was like that of the stars compared to the sunlight that we enjoy from God's revealed word. In those lands normally there were none belonging to the dispensation of the Holy Spirit, or even to the dispensation of the Son. But it seems not unreasonable to believe that there were many in the dispensation of the Father.

In the revelation we have in the Scriptures it is made clear that God is seeking men. The shepherd seeks his lost sheep; the father awaits with eager and sorrowing heart the return of the lost son. Among the heathen this comforting fact is not known, and one of the most pathetic things in the world is the fact that many of the heathen are blindly groping after God, and even when a solution for their troubles is offered they do not recognize it as such. If they make an honest and earnest effort to be true to the highest and best that they know we believe that our heavenly Father will recognize them as belonging to His fold.   But, someone may say that Jesus is the door, and those who would enter in any other way are thieves and robbers.   That is perfectly true.   There is no other way.   But it is a source of vast satisfaction that we do not have to know the name of the door.   In the light that is ours we have the privilege of knowing the name of the door and much other important and satisfying knowledge thereof.   But we may rejoice that the door is not closed to those who do not have this information, provided they come even with faltering step, groping their way through the darkness to the door that furnishes entrance to the larger life.

Some in this land may question the wisdom of sending the gospel to the heathen if there is a possibility of salvation for them without the revealed gospel that we have.   This would not be questioned by one who is himself in the dispensation of the Son, or of the Holy Spirit, and who in addition has a knowledge of actual conditions in the heathen lands.   We know too well the infinite satisfaction of living in these higher stages of religious experience to hesitate for a moment to extend these privileges to all people everywhere, even unto the uttermost parts of the world.

Another thing that we might note in this connection is the restraining influence of the Holy Spirit against the forces of evil.   But for that restraint none of us could imagine the horrors that might engulf the world. Sometimes that restraint for purposes of His own is partially withdrawn by God, as at present, and we realize into what a terrible condition Hitler and those like-minded can bring the world. The restraint of the Holy Spirit may be exerted directly, or through human personalities who have yielded themselves to Him. In heathen lands much of this restraint is lacking, and as a result they have a low and debased civilization. There is probably no one among us who has any proper appreciation of the tremendous influence of the Spirit-filled life. Much is possible even in the case of a very saintly man in the dispensation of the Father as we see in the case of Abraham pleading for Sodom. How much more is it true in the case of one who is in the dispensation of the Son, and more especially still of one who is in the dispensation of the Holy Ghost.

DIVORCE

There is much confusion of thought in the Christian world as to divorce. As we consider the words of Christ it appears to be so plain and simple that it would seem absurd for anyone to call it a complicated question. And yet when we get just below surface thinking we realize that it is not so simple. That the world might be populated and repopulated the marriage of one man to one woman—"so long as they both shall live"—was God's plan to be followed throughout the ages.

In addition to other reasons the little human babies have a long period of helplessness during which the co-operation of both father and mother is needed. In addition to the care of physical needs there must be mental and spiritual development for which a wholesome home life is important if not absolutely necessary.

So it is perfectly clear that this is God's plan and that
He has no other. Christ mentioned only one exception
—adultery. We may remember that in describing
adultery on another occasion He included thought as
well as deed. That in itself would bring much com-
plexity. Then, too, adultery is often one of the main
causes of divorce, but because of the difficulty of getting adequate proof some other cause is given. But incidentally He in answer to a question mentioned another circumstance that in many of our discussions we
entirely overlook, that is, the attitude of Moses on the
subject. The Jews in actual practice were very lax
with regard to divorce, the men especially being permitted to divorce the wife for almost any cause. One
famous group, the School of Hillel, went so far as to declare it a sufficient ground for divorce if a wife spoiled
her husband's dinner.

Now there existed in the time of Moses the same ob-
jections to divorce that existed in the time of Jesus, and
that exist today. Why was Moses so lenient as he was?
Jesus said it was because of the "hardness of their
hearts." That is, so many of the Jews were of such low
spiritual vitality that as a law maker Moses simply
could not be over-strict in the matter of divorce.

What of the situation in our land today? If everyone
were in the dispensation of the Holy Spirit or even in
the dispensation of the Son there would scarcely be
any need for divorce laws. It is where one or both are
either living sinful lives, or at best are in the dispensation of the Father, that practically all divorces occur.
The law-maker today must consider this element just
as Moses did. The law should be just as strict as the

spiritual condition of the people will permit. To do more than that would bring about a condition worse than divorce. The only permanent remedy for divorce is a deeper spirituality among the people. The place to be strict is at marriage. There could scarcely be found a more objectionable condition than that found in one State—almost no restrictions in marriage, and no divorce at all.

SUFFERING

This is a world of suffering. People are constantly asking why it is so. Why did God make such a world, and why does He continue to permit it? And we often make it personal, and ask in plaintive voice why God does not do better by us. This subject is entirely too big to be treated here except in outline, and to illustrate the value of the higher spiritual dispensations in connection with it.

In a general way there are four classes of suffering:

1. Those caused directly by our own weakness, ignorance, or sin.

2. From causes for which we individually are not responsible, as storms, infantile paralysis, etc.

3. Vicarious suffering—involuntary. That is, suffering on account of others, not willingly, but from necessity, as from a drunken father, a sinful world.

4. Vicarious suffering—voluntary. That is, suffering for others and doing it willingly and even gladly because we are constrained to do so because of love, as a mother spending wakeful days and nights over a sick child; a missionary leaving home and friends for painful burden-bearing in a strange land, and often among

a thoroughly unappreciative people. Let us consider
these a little more fully.

1. A man is lazy and he has to do without many
things that the industrious may have. Another man
gets on a drunken spree and a bursting headache follows. A woman makes and spreads untrue and unkind
stories about her neighbors, and she has no friends.
If breaking the laws of nature and of God did not bring
suffering what would be the result? Suppose I carelessly or thoughtlessly put my hand on a red hot stove
and suffering did not warn of the danger. My hand
would be burned off and I would be crippled for life.
Instead of complaining about the pain that causes me
to jerk my hand away quickly I should thank God that
a slight pain saves me from a much greater one. Or if
an unrighteous gratification of appetite or passion were
not followed with painful consequences the peoples of
the world would doubtless soon become in large measure a mass of moral and physical rottenness. We should
profoundly thank God that in this way He is making
every possible effort to save us from the results of our
own sins.

It is not difficult for a thoughtful mind to grasp the
above. But the other three classes bring greater difficulties to most people. Sinful people cannot understand it at all. Those in the dispensation of the Father
understand it so imperfectly that often the best they
can do is to endure affliction with grim stoicism. But
as we come into the dispensation of the Son, and especially into the dispensation of the Holy Ghost we
can begin to see things as Jesus saw them, and what
seemed dark and hard before become not only clear

and understandable but even beneficent and valuable.

There is no virtue in suffering of itself. But it pricks the bubble of our self-importance and self-sufficiency, and thus puts us in a condition where God can help us. This is aptly illustrated by the following story told by Lieutenant Colonel Warren J. Clear of his experience in Bataan:

In this fighting many a soldier came to realize that self-confidence alone was not enough to sustain the human spirit. "I remember jumping into a hole during a particularly heavy bombing attack. A sergeant crouched lower to make room for me. Then all hell broke loose, and I wasn't surprised to find myself praying out loud. I heard the sergeant praying too. When the attack was over I said:

"Sergeant, I noticed you were praying."

"Yes sir," he answered, without batting an eye, "there are no atheists in foxholes."

There is a passage in the Bible that comes to us first as a great shock. It is this: "Jesus, the Captain of our salvation, was made perfect through suffering." How can this be? Jesus was always perfect. No stain of sin ever touched Him. No sting of conscience ever disturbed his rest. But we must remember that we not only have a relationship with God, but with our fellowmen also, and we are under obligation to lift them to God to the extent of our ability and opportunity. That was true also of Jesus. He was perfect in character. But He could not lift the world to God without suffering. His sufferings, not on his own account, but for our sakes has touched the heart of the world. It was not easy for Him as it is not easy for us. But as we come into the higher dispensations especially into that of the Holy Spirit we are able to pray that most wonderful of all prayers, that we may have not only the power of His resurrection, but also the fellowship of His suffering.

This much we should add in this condition. Suffering simply cannot be understood if this life is all. If we believe in a good God we must believe in a life beyond the grave. If we regard this life as a short period in which we are fitted for companionship with God and all the good throughout a vast eternity, then suffering as one of the chief agencies in that great task becomes understandable and explainable.

PRAYER

No one ever goes to God with an earnest, honest plea without receiving a kindly hearing. Once when Jesus was passing through Samaria a poor sinful woman found in Him an answer to the cry of her heart. She carried the good news to the city. Crowds came out and were so stirred at His majesty and His speech that they "besought Him that He would tarry with them, and He abode there two days." We believe that there is living evidence of that visit even to this day in the small group of Samaritans who are still followers of the Nazarene. On another occasion He was in the country of the Gadarenes. He cast the devils out of a demoniac. At the entreaty of the demons he permitted them to enter into a herd of swine. The swine rushed into the sea and were drowned. Now the people, more anxious to have their swine than Jesus, "began to pray to Him to depart out of their coasts." He answered their request and left them.   The privilege of prayer entails upon us also a tremendous responsibility.   In a sense what we want most is what we are praying for regardless of the words we utter.   All unconsciously to ourselves we often pray contradictory prayers.   A man prays for money and the success of his business, and at the same time prays that he may be a good man and his family faithful and true.   Both prayers, it may be are uttered in faith, subject only to the will of God. It may well be that God may see as the man cannot that the attainment of large business success may mean leanness of soul for himself or family.   In a case like that God loves to answer the larger prayer—the prayer that will have the largest returns throughout eternity.

In the lower spiritual ranges the prayers are apt to be very largely of a selfish nature for the material and physical needs of ourselves and our immediate family. Nationally many are far more concerned for peace than for righteousness, overlooking the fact that a durable peace is always a by-product of righteousness.

In the dispensation of the Son we begin to have a serious concern for others.   In the dispensation of the Holy Spirit that becomes so pronounced that one is willing to endure great privations and sufferings through extended periods in behalf of others.   In this state one's prayers in large measure cease to be appeals to God for things, but becomes rather a matter of companionship with God.   Jesus spent many hours in prayer—not begging the Father for things, but talking with Him as friend with friend.   Jesus had a task of great difficulty.   It was a great relief to Him to talk it all over with His Father.   So it is with us only in a much more limited way. We have our problems and difficulties. It helps wonderfully in our prayers to talk over everything with God. We may want something very much, but we leave it to Him to determine whether it is best for us. It may help us to remember that He refused to grant the most earnest prayer of His greatest servant. Paul had a thorn in the flesh—many think it was serious eye trouble. He besought the Lord thrice that it might depart from him. God did not grant the request, but said, "My grace shall be sufficient for thee." So it is always. If God withholds something from us, He always gives us something better instead. We are helping God do His work, and so He obligates Himself to furnish sufficient material. Having such a partner relieves us of many worries and fears.

SOCIAL LIFE

One of our most difficult problems becomes more rather than less difficult the more "advanced" we become. I mean our social life, especially that of unmarried young people. Preachers ought to be leaders in this, but with occasional exceptions they are not. In most cases it is not because they do not see the need, or are not anxious to meet it, but rather because the difficulties are so great that they feel helpless to do anything out of the ordinary.

There is in the minds of many young people, and old ones, too, for that matter, the belief that the more pious people are the less sympathy they have for this sort of thing. This is not true at all. If the world continues to be populated people must marry. There are perfectly good reasons why some people do not marry. But these are the exceptions. The natural order is for young people to marry. That being so it is of great importance that every proper and reasonable encouragement be given to young people of opposite sex to meet and mingle in a wholesome and happy way, for the double reason that the young people enjoy it, and because in this way matings may be made that are happier and more suitable.

It is interesting to note that at the very beginning of His public ministry Jesus was present at the marriage festivities of a young couple, very likely some of His kinsfolk from the fact that His mother took such an active part, and when the happiness of the occasion was about to be marred He performed a miracle to prevent it.

The word "compassion" was used frequently of Christ. He had compassion on these young people and He did something about it. The closer we are to Jesus the more anxious we are to be helpful in this way as well as in other ways. Here is an opportunity for consecrated womanhood that is particularly appealing, and it takes real consecration to get rid of the snobbery of artificial distinctions that constitutes the chief hindrance here.

The camp meetings of the nineteenth century played a mighty part in making this country what it is. We have heard much of their spiritual atmosphere and influence, and the value and importance of this can scarcely be exaggerated. But the social values of the camp meetings have not generally been appreciated at their true worth. Not only great spiritual decisions were made, but social contacts and marital pledges were made here that helped to make this country a land of happy homes.

Later, protracted meetings in country churches during the summer with dinner on the grounds served a double function—religious and social. But they did not equal the camp meeting. Today conditions have made those occasions generally impracticable. And in our city churches, whether among poor or rich, nothing of a very satisfactory sort has been developed in their place. To leave a matter of such vital importance to commercial exploitation is a most unworthy shirking of responsibility. But, fortunately, we do not have to think of doing this as a duty so much as a delightful privilege. We are hoping that because of the urgency of the need a solution or a series of solutions may be evolved.

It is important that the three basic human needs shall be met: Food, pleasant and wholesome contacts between the sexes, and earnest, honest and sincere appeals for holier living. If we can devise ways to accomplish these things in a large or small way we will help forward the Kingdom of God.

WAR

Is it ever right to engage in war? There are some sincere people who do not think so. For the most part their trouble lies in their failure to understand the facts brought out in this book, that there are three dispensations, and that many people in our own land and nearly everybody in some lands are either in rebellion against God, or if they may claim to be religious at all, have never gotten beyond the dispensation of the Father. If the great majority of the peoples of all the nations were in the dispensation of the Son or of the Holy Spirit there would be no war.

The spirit and attitude of Jesus are entirely against war, yet He did not oppose war. Never once did He advise His followers to refuse to go to war; never once did He censure a soldier because of his occupation. On the contrary He frankly stated that wars would continue. In the Old Testament period people did not question the wisdom of some wars. In fact, God's people on many occasions were particularly ordered to engage in war. Those conditions still prevailed when Jesus was on earth. While the conditions are better in some lands now than when Jesus came—and better because He came—nevertheless the great majority of the peoples of the earth do not now have the Christian spirit and understanding. Until they do have, wars will be inevitable. But some people are so obsessed with the thought that peace is the greatest good, they insist that anything that would disturb the peace of individuals or nations is bad. But such a position cannot be sustained at all. There is an inner peace that Jesus gives all His followers. Nothing can take that away. But they are not talking of that. They are talking of the outward peace. And that is not the greatest good at all. The greatest good is righteousness. Jesus never held up peace as a worthy objective. It was always righteousness. He did not have outward peace Himself. His enemies fought Him in every way they dared. And He fought back, or would have if that crowd had not been too cowardly to fight. He took a cord and drove them out of the temple. Someone has said, "Might till right is ready." And that is not our choice in many cases. Necessity is laid upon us. We must either fight or lose what we cherish more than life. And if we are fighting for righteousness and in the right spirit we may be assured that our action will have the approval of God.

The thing that Jesus opposed was not war, but hate. Hate is bad in time of war, or in time of peace. It is not necessary in either. In our war between the States there seemed to be a marked freedom from hate in Lee and Jackson on the Southern side and of Lincoln and Grant on the Northern side, and these were the men who have won and kept in a most remarkable way the affections of all the people, and those who rise above hate, even while fighting for righteousness, are rendering the world in their way a noble service. Much of the confusion on this phase of the subject comes from a confusion of terms. There is such a thing as hate and there is such a thing as righteous indignation, and they are very different. But some people never seem to find it out. No normal person can see a big bully cruelly beat a little child and not be indignant, and it certainly is of the righteous variety. This may apply to all individuals and to nations. And to see such injustice and not do what we reasonably can about it is something that any true man should be ashamed of. Hate on the contrary hurts us within and unfits us for rendering the largest service.

GRATITUDE

We hear in the course of ordinary conversation a good deal about gratitude, and by common consent one who shows a marked lack of gratitude for favors received is an object of almost universal censure. This is an indication of the exalted place gratitude has in our thinking.

What occasion have we for gratitude, especially to God? When we consider an answer to that question we very naturally think of material blessings, such as food, clothing, shelter, financial ease, friends, and pleasant living conditions. But gratitude cannot be determined by the abundance and quality of these at all. Some who have almost everything weary their friends with their complaints, while some of those who are but scantily supplied with the necessities of life are happy because of their overflowing gratitude to God.

Some years ago Alice Hegan Rice wrote a delightful little book on "Mrs. Wiggs of the Cabbage Patch." Mrs. Wiggs lived with her childen in a shanty in the "Cabbage Patch," a seemingly God-forsaken section of a big city, and in spite of her abject poverty was radiant with gratitude. She said that not being afflicted with a harelip was enough to keep one happy. The clothes of her children were pretty well covered with patches, and sometimes the colors of the patches in front and behind did not harmonize, but she said that did not matter because no one ever saw them coming and going at the same time anyway. And so she walked with majestic tread through a man-cursed section of the earth.

As we ascend the spiritual stairway we get farther and farther away from the thralldom of the material, and reach out into the illimitable horizons of mind and spirit.

But how many of us reach the highest landing place of the spiritual stairway in the matter of gratitude? To answer that we need to go back farther and ask what is the highest attainment for us. Is it not that we be like God? Or is such an idea too preposterous even to be considered? But we are assured in God's word that the idea is not preposterous at all, but that in deed and in truth God has made us in His own image and after His own likeness. In view of that fact is not the highest form of gratitude the simple recognition and wholehearted appreciation of that favor? How greatly we have been honored in this way is beyond the power of the human mind to conceive. We may get some idea by comparison with the angels, for they are God's messengers, but we are to be His friends and companions forever. In contemplation of that honor should we consider it a hard thing that He should expect us to spend this life in preparation for that high and holy companionship throughout the endless ages of eternity?

We have appropriated from the French an expression, "noblesse oblige," that has special meaning here. In the period when different classes were recognized and legalized in France the nobility enjoyed many special privileges. In grateful acknowledgment that they were born into the nobility, and enjoyed a higher social status, and were therefore the recipients of so many and so great privileges there was an acknowledged feeling that in return they were obligated on their part to render such services as they could to those less favored. But most of the French nobility did not live worthy of that expression. There was a time when there was a terrific conflict in France between the higher spiritual elements and the lower. The lower won. They slew their prophets and killed those who might have saved them, and with gay abandon great numbers of them drifted into atheism. They are now reaping the results. It would seem that nothing but suffering would save them. It seems peculiarly sad that the masses of the people have been sacrificed by the ambition and selfishness of their leaders.

It is easy enough to criticise the French, and especially their leaders. How is it with us in the realm of the spirit? Shall we be grateful to God above all else that He has made us like Himself? If so, are we not under special obligation to live like Him? What does it mean to live like Him? Fortunately, we are not left in the dark here. Jesus not only told us how God lives, He showed us. The record of His life furnishes the goal to which we should aspire.

But here is the heart of much of the world's troubles. Most of us do not want to live too much like Jesus. Even men noted for their piety do not find it easy. It is easier to drift with the crowd than to face criticism, loss of high position or a voluntary surrender of the hope and expectation of attaining such position. Jesus came, as He Himself tells us, not to be ministered unto but to minister. But that doesn't suit most of us. We want other folks to wait on us. He suffered every humiliation his foes could bestow upon Him. He suffered physical pain even unto death while still a young man. As we consider this should it seem a hard thing for a man to lose a high position, and in a sense be ostracised, if the cause of truth should make that necessary? Any true man will want to be sure he is right, and that he is obeying God before he takes a position that may bring poverty, humiliation, and heartache to his family.

And yet many men face that situation every day. Will they compromise or will they yield themselves entirely to the will of God? The question may be easier if we give serious consideration to the testimonies given on previous pages showing that a complete surrender will revolutionize individual lives and through them often untold numbers of others.

Paul said: "If we suffer we shall also reign with Him. If we deny Him, He will also deny us." Commenting on this passage, Mrs. Howard Taylor, one of the great women of the world whose suffering for China has helped to bring about the marvelous changes there said: "We will have an eternity in which to worship God, we have only this life in which to suffer for Him."

THE TRAIL OF BURNING HEARTS

How burning hearts kindle and perpetuate spiritual fires throughout all lands constitutes one of the most interesting fields of historical research. One may begin almost anywhere and go backward and forward and be rewarded with thrilling revelations of divine accomplishment. John Wickliffe translated the Bible into English, and was a faithful evangelical preacher. Because of unusual conditions he did not lose his life as many others before and after him did. His work and message became known in Germany and lodged in the heart of John Huss, who became a vigorous preacher and had many followers. His enemies burned his body at the stake and imagined it was all over. But years later a small group of his followers, mostly plain people, warmed the heart of John Wesley. A little later this heart became a glowing flame and started untold thousands of fires in throbbing human hearts. Two plain women, who had caught the fire from Wesley's preachers, kindled the fire in Moody's heart, and through him countless thousands of others have been touched. Again, one hundred years after Wyckliffe, William Tyndale was born. The work of Wyckliffe so inspired him that he determined to make a translation better suited to the needs of the plain peole, and, the printing press having been in the meantime invented, to make them cheap enough in price so the boy at the plow could have a copy. It cost him his life, but how he made one of the three greatest translations of all time, his translation being the basis of our present beautiful New Testament, and having a vast deal to do with the formation and development of our virile English language, is well known.

Consider our foreign mission work. John Newton, of Olney was a friend and correspondent of Wesley and shared with him the new baptism. Newton communicated the divine fire to Thomas Scott, up to that time by his own confession, a formalist clergyman with no experience of the Spirit's grace in his heart. A young man in his congregation, Wm. Cary, was powerfully quickened and became one of the world's greatest missionaries. There strayed into his congregation another young man, Claudius Buchanan, who a few years later went to India as a missionary. He published a tract, "The Star in the East," which crossing the ocean fell into the hands of Adoniram Judson, then a student at Andover, and influenced him to give his life to foreign missions.

The illustrations given above have been of men of modern times. But the experience has been for all time. None, perhaps, is quite so impressive as that with the Master and two of His disciples on the afternoon of the resurrection as they walked from Jerusalem to Emmaus, some seven or eight miles. St. Luke tells the beautiful story. Luke 24:13-32.

13. And, behold, two of them went that same day to a village called Emmaus, which was from Jerusalem about threescore furlongs.

14. And they talked together of all those things which had happened.

15. And it came to pass that, while they communed together and reasoned, Jesus Himself drew near, and went with them.

16. But their eyes were holden that they should not know Him.

17. And He said unto them, What manner of communications are these, that ye have one to another, as ye walk, and are sad?

18. And the one of them, whose name was Cleopas, answering said unto him, Art thou only a stranger in Jerusalem, and hast not known the things which are come to pass there in these days?

19. And he said unto them, What things? and they said unto him, Concerning Jesus of Nazareth, which was a prophet mighty in deed and word before God and all the people:

20. And how the chief priests and our rulers delivered him to be condemned to death, and have crucified him.

21. But we trusted that it had been he which

should have redeemed Israel: and beside all this, today is the third day since these things were done.

22.   Yea, and certain women also of our company made us astonished, which were early at the sepulchre;

23.   And when they found not his body, they came, saying, that they had also seen a vision of angels, which said that he was alive.

24.   And certain of them which were with us went to the sepulchre, and found it even so as the women had said; but him they saw not.

25.   Then he said unto them, O fools, and slow of heart to believe all that the prophets have spoken:

26.   Ought not Christ to have suffered these things, and to enter into his glory?

27.   And beginning at Moses and all the prophets, he expounded unto them in all the Scriptures the things concerning himself.

28.   And they drew nigh unto the village, whither they went. and he made as though he would have gone further.

29.   But they constrained him, saying, Abide with us; for it is toward evening, and the day is far spent, and he went in to tarry with them.

30.   And it came to pass, as he sat at meat with them, he took bread, and blessed it, and brake, and gave to them.

31.   And their eyes were opened, and they knew him; and he vanished out of their sight.

32.   And they said one to another, Did not our heart burn within us, while he talked with us by the way, and while he opened to us the Scriptures?

So it has gone, and so may it continue to go.   May

our hearts catch the divine flame and so carry it on that those who follow us may rejoice that we too have been torchbearers for God.

THE END

INDEX

www.ingramcontent.com/pod-product-compliance
Lightning Source LLC
Chambersburg PA
CBHW031952040426
42448CB00006B/327